A Journey through 100 Years of Indian Cinema

Cinema Quiz Book

Saumya Chaki

Address
BH 170, Sector 2, Salt Lake
Kolkata - 700091 (Near Tank no. 7)

ISBN: 978-93-84333-86-7

First Published: November 2014

Price: ₹250/-

Cover Design
Tisha Mukherjee

Distributed by

purushottam-bookstore.com
power-publishers.com
infibeam.com
crossword.in
flipkart.com
ebay.in

TABLE OF CONTENTS

Introduction

Indian cinema is the largest movie industry on our planet. We have the most diverse movies shot in a large number of regional languages as well as Hindi and English. While there have been numerous articles on Indian cinema, there appears to be a limited number of books written on Indian cinema. This realization strikes a stronger chord as we complete a centenary of Indian films starting with a humble beginning in the films of silent era. If we look at the prevailing literature on Indian cinema it is either devoted to making of cult films like Sholay, or biographies of leading film personalities like directors, actors, music directors. It is interesting to note that we have very few quiz books on Indian cinema. This brings us to the birth of this attempt to capture some interesting facets of Indian cinema through a quiz book. Being an avid quizzer, I have attended numerous quiz events across the country. I found that in most quizzes, there are limited sections devoted on Indian films. Given this background and my old weakness for quizzing (from school days) I researched on the history of Indian cinema (Hindi, Bengali and other major regional language films like Marathi, Gujarati, Tamil, Telegu, Kannada, Malayalam and Oriya) and how these industries have evolved in the past 100 years. English films made in India have also been covered in this book. Our films have come a long way from the silent era to the age of talkies and playback singing. So sit back on your sofa or arm chair and put on your thinking caps as we embark on a journey of Indian films over the last 100 years. The book is divided into 10 chapters and has more than 650 questions on films shot over the last 100 years in diverse languages. This book I believe will be useful to quizzers and anyone with an interest in Indian films. Anyone with an interest in Indian films, be it a student of cinema or an average film buff or even a quizzer would find this book interesting. It is my humble attempt to bring out some interesting facets of Indian films and rekindle memories of some long gone men and women who played a pivotal role in what constitutes the Indian film industry today.

Happy quizzing!!

Saumya Chaki

October 31st, 2014

Chapter One - Indian Cinema, a Centenary of Ideas

1   Indian Cinema – a centenary of ideas

Indian cinema completed a century in 2013. The centenary was marked by special events celebrating cinema over the last century. Books were written and films like 'Bombay Talkies' were made to celebrate the achievements and growth of Indian cinema. Given this back drop it is rather interesting to note that there are not too many quiz books on Indian cinema. Being a film buff I felt it would be my small attempt to bridge this gap. As an author I am not gifted with an education or background in films, neither do I profess to be a critic. The idea behind this book is to create more interest about the journey of Indian films and recognize the work of eminent directors and actors.

This book is structured into 10 chapters – Chapter 1 being an Introduction, Chapter 2 covers Hindi cinema, Chapter 3 covers Bengali cinema, Chapter 4 covers Regional language cinema, Chapter 5 covers Indian films at film festivals abroad and in India, Chapter 6 covers Film Awards in India, Chapter 7 covers Indian cinema at the Oscars, Chapter 8 covers Indian cinema made in English and Chapter 9 has a general movie quiz with multiple choice questions, Chapter 10 has all the answers to the questions in Chapters 2 to 9.

This book covers Hindi cinema in chapter 2 in three sections – the Early Years that start from the beginning with Raja Harishchandra to the pre-Independence years, followed by Movies after 1947 that covers movies till the end of the 20th century and then the New Millennium cinema (2000 onwards).

Bengali cinema is covered in chapter three and cuts across the entire spectrum of the initial silent years moving on to the talkies and the golden period of Uttam Kumar – Suchitra Sen and the splendid work of Satyajit Ray, Mrinal Sen, Buddhadeb Dasgupta, Tapan Sinha and Ritwik Ghatak and finally on to new age cinema that brings promise of new creativity and modern subjects through the work of Aparna Sen, Sandip Ray, Srijit Mukherjee, Aniruddha Roy Chowdhury and others.

Regional movies have been covered in chapter four a cover a wide spectrum of languages like Tamil, Malayalam, Kannada, Telegu, Oriya, Assamese, Gujarati and Marathi cinema. The cinematic adventures of directors like Shankar Nag, Mani Ratnam, Adoor Gopalakrishnan and others have added flavours and layers of cinematic expression.

Chapter five deals with Indian films at film festivals over the years including Cannes, Berlin and Moscow. Chapter six covers film awards in India including National Film Awards, state film awards, Dada Saheb Phalke Awards and Filmfare awards. Chapter seven covers Indian cinema at the Oscars including the nominations and winners. Chapter eight covers Indian cinema made in English which has also evolved over the years with many innovative scripts helped by Indian writing in English as well. Chapter nine covers a general movie quiz with multiple choice questions. Chapter ten covers all the answers from chapters 2 to 9.

I have also included two appendices – Appendix A on the winners of Dada Saheb Phalke award till 2014 and Appendix B on some leading directors of Indian cinema. The list is not exhaustive and is limited to the author's knowledge of cinema.

I attempt to bring out some interesting facts about Indian cinema and its unique journey of 100 years through this quiz book. For instance did you know that one of the leading actresses in Bollywood in the 1970's was also a top notch NCC cadet during the Republic Day parade in New Delhi. Or could you name the first Hindi film to be crowd sourced from social networks? I only hope my readers who attempt to read this book and test their knowledge of Indian cinema, would enjoy this journey of film facts as much as I enjoyed researching and collating them.

The Early Years

Indian cinema started way back in 1913 with the legendary 'Raja Harishchandra'. The silent years were marked by a period of struggle for the pioneers in getting finance, actors to play diverse roles and a limited market for cinema. Way back in 1913, in Nasik, a small town near Nagpur, a devout man sold his wife's jewellery, pledged his insurance policies, to produce and direct the first movie made in India by an Indian. His name was Dhundiraj Govind Phalke, better known as Dadasaheb Phalke. This marked the remarkable journey of Indian cinema. The inspiration for making this film came to Phalke when he watched 'Life of Christ' in 1911. He was keen to see Indian images on screen in a local production. The next year marked the start of shooting for Raja Harishchandra at a studio in Dadar. The film was completed in 1912 and released at the Coronation Cinema on April 21, 1913. Some other well known films of the silent era include – Shri Krishna Janma (1918), Sant Tukaram (1921), Sant Namdev (1922), and Bhakt Prahlad (1926).

Time to put on the thinking caps! The next few chapters deal with quizzes from films all over India.

Chapter Two − Hindi Movies Quiz

2 Hindi Movies Quiz

2.1 The Early Years

Questions -

1) What was India's first movie with a sound track?

2) What was special about the date March 14, 1931?

3) What was common to the films Miss Frontier Mail (1936) and Punjab Mail (1939)?

4) Who founded Bombay Talkies in 1934?

5) This actress was considered the 'first sex symbol of Indian Cinema' and went on to win the Dadasaheb Phalke award? Who is she?

6) Which was the first Hindi movie to use playback singing?

7) Which was the first colour movie made in Hindi?

8) Who was known as the 'Paul Muni of India'?

9) Name the first Indian film to be screened at an International Film festival?

10) This doyen of Hindi cinema and theatre played a key role in Sikander (1941) and later went on to win the Dada Saheb Phalke Award. Who was he?

11) Name the leading pair in the iconic film 'Acchot Kanya'?

12) Who was Ashok Kumar's co-star in 'Izzat' shot in 1937?

13) What was K L Saigal's debut movie?

14) Who starred as Devdas in the 1935 film 'Devdas'?

15) This director started as an actor in Apradhi in 1931. He went on to direct films like Devdas, Manzil and Mukti. Who is he?

16) Who played the role of Veena in Hindustan Hamara?

17) Who composed the music for the film 'Zindagi' shot in 1940?

18) One of the finest exponents of Rabindra Sangeet, he also composed music in Hindi and Bengali films. He went on to win the Dada Saheb Phalke award. Who is he?

19) What was Hemant Kumar's first Hindi film as a singer?

20) Which movie directed by Raj Kapoor won the Crystal Globe award at the Karlovy Vary International Film Festival?

21) Inquilab (1935) was his first film. He later went on to star with Nargis in many films. Name this iconic actor?

22) He has been described as the 'ultimate method actor' by Satyajit Ray. He made his debut in Jwar Bhatta in 1944. He was later awarded the Dada Saheb Phalke Award. Name this iconic actor?

23) She acted as a child artist in Jwar Bhatta. Later she acted in both Hindi and Bengali films. She was also an exponent of Rabindra Sangeet. Name this actress?

24) He made his debut in the film Shikari (1946). He later went on to act in both Hindi and Bengali films

and won 9 Film Fare Awards for Best Male Playback Singer. Name the actor cum singer?

25) This leading actress was known as 'the first lady of Indian Cinema'. She debut in the movie Karma and later became the recipient of Dada Saheb Phalke Award. Name the actress?

26) This bilingual film made in Hindi and English was the first Indian film to feature an onscreen kiss. The story involved a princess falling in love with a neighbouring prince. Name this movie?

27) She was trained in Hindustani classic music and later sang in All India Radio with her sister in the 1920's. She later became one of first woman composers in Bollywood. Name this talented singer cum composer?

28) This iconic Hindi film directed by Sohrab Modi and starring Prithviraj Kapoor was based on the life of Alexander. Name this movie?

29) Her real name was Ruby Myers. She worked as a telephone operator before she joined films. She became the highest paid actress of her time. Later she was awarded Dada Saheb Phalke Award. Name this actress?

30) He acted in Parsi theatre and later became an actor, director in Hindi films. His significant work included Khoon Ka Khoon, Sikander, Pukar, Jhansi Ki Rani. Name this director cum actor?

31) This music director debuted with the movie 'Prem Nagar (1940)'. He brought in the concept of sound mixing in Hindi films. He later went on to win the Dada Saheb Phalke Award. Name this award winning music director?

32) She lost her father at 13. She went on to become one of iconic playback singers in Hindi films. She held the world record for most recordings in the Guinness Book of World Records from 1974 to 1991. She was conferred the Bharat Ratna in 2001. Who is she?

33) He penned his first song for Shahjehan (1946) and went on to compose music for over 350 Hindi films. Name this iconic lyricist?

34) This 1941 movie was the debut film of actor Bharat Bhusan. It was also one of top grossing Hindi films in 1941. Later this movie was remade in 1964. Name this film?

35) This actress starred in the 1944 film 'Rattan'. She later moved to Pakistan after partition and worked in Pakistani cinema. Name this actress?

36) He was born in Burdwan district, Bengal. He was a well known director of the 1940's and 1950's. He directed films like Apna Ghar (1942) and Nartaki (1940). Name this director?

37) He was born in Madhya Pradesh. He made his debut in V.Shantaram's 'Amrit Manthan' and played the role of Emperor Jehangir in Pukar. Name this talented actor?

38) Who composed the music for the Hindi film Roti (1942)?

39) Who played the role of Badshah Humayun in the 1945 film 'Humayun' directed by Mehboob Khan?

40) She was born in Calcutta. She started her career as a child artist in Talashe Haq (1935). Later she became one of big stars of Hindi cinema and won many awards including the Padma Shri. Who is she?

2.2 Movies after 1947 – this section covers Hindi films made in the period 1948 to 1999.

Questions –

1) Who was the first Indian actress to win Best Actress award in an International Festival?

2) Which Bollywood movie features retired General VK Singh in a cameo role?

3) Who is the first Indian movie star to be featured on the cover of Time magazine?

4) Chupke Chupke is the copy of which Bengali film?

5) Who composed music for the movie Solva Saal (1958)?

6) Who played the mouth organ in the song 'Mere Sapno Ki Rani' from the film Aradhana (1969)?

7) Who directed the film 'Badhti ka naam Daari'?

8) Which Hindi film was shot at Air Force Academy near Hyderabad?

9) What is common to the Shyam Benegal's movies Manthan and Susman?

10) Who won the National Film Award for Best Supporting Actor for the film Drohkaal?

11) Which Indian cricketer starred in the movie 'Kabhi Ajnabee The' with Poonam Dhillon?

12) Which is the only Hindi movie made on the Sino-India war of 1962?

13) Who played the role of Shivnath Sharma in the movie Bawarchi?

14) Who directed the movie 'Kisi Se Na Kehna'?

15) Who won the National Film Award for Best Actor for the movie Bhuvan Shome?

16) This Bollywood superstar made his debut in the film 'Aakhri Khat'?

17) Who won his first Filmfare Award for the song 'Roop Tera Mastana'?

18) Who played the role of Sulekha Chaturvedi in the film 'Chupke Chupke'?

19) Ritwik Ghatak introduced this actor into films. He was known for comic drunkard roles in films like 'Golmaal'.

20) This actor portrayed character roles and was a member of Mumbai's Bene Isreal community. He won the Filmfare Best Supporting Actor award in 1955 for his work in Boot Polish.

21) He studied at Sherwood College, Nainital. He went on to make his debut as a narrator in Mrinal Sen's 'Bhuvan Shome'. He went on to become one of the most celebrated actors in Bollywood and won 3 National Awards for Best Actor. Name this iconic actor?

22) She was born in Jabalpur. She won the best NCC cadet award in the 1966 Republic Day Celebrations. She went on to study at FTII, Pune. She has won 3 National Film Awards for Best Actress. Name this renowned actress?

23) What is common to Mithun Chakraborty, Rakesh Bedi, Shabana Azmi and Satish Kaushik?

24) Son of a leading film director of the 1980's, he played the lead role of Peter D'souza in the film Prahaar. Name the actor?

25) He was a well known comic actor in films like 'Rang Birangi' and 'Chasme Badoor'. He went on to win the National Film Award for Best Supporting Actor in 2010. Name this talented actor?

26) He directed some iconic movies like 'Gol Maal', 'Guddi'. He was known to make movies involving middle class subjects. He was awarded the Dada Saheb Phalke Award in 1999. Name this well known Bollywood director?

27) He studied chemistry at Scottish Church College, Kolkata. He studied at FTII, Pune and went on to win the National Film Award for his debut film in 1976. Name the actor?

28) Who wrote the screenplay for Raj Kapoor's classic film 'Mera Naam Joker?

29) Name two Hindi films to have 2 intervals?

30) He was one of the leading actors of Bollywood from late 1940's to 1960's. He directed and produced films as well. He won 2 National Awards and 9 Filmfare Awards. Name this renowned actor and director?

31) This war film featured the war fought between British Indian forces and Japanese forces in Burma. Mala Sinha played the role of Usha Choudhury in this film. Name the film?

32) Who played the role of a British Indian Army officer Major Ram Kapoor in the 1972 film 'Lalkaar'?

33) What was common to the films Raja Jani, Seeta Aur Geeta, Jugnu, Charas and Sholay?

34) This film is set in the background of civil war in Uganda. It was directed by Ramanand Sagar. Name this film?

35) He won the Filmfare Award for Best Director for the film Guide and Filmfare Award for Best Editing for the film Johnny Mera Naam. Name this well known director?

36) Who sang the duet 'Charas-Charas' from the film Charas?

37) This iconic composer duo composed music for over 600 Hindi films between 1963 and 1998. They won 7 Filmfare Awards. Name this duo?

38) Who won the Filmfare Award for Best Supporting Actress for the film 'Meri Jung'?

39) He was born in Chembur, Mumbai. He became a well known actor in Hindi films. He has now ventured in Hollywood films and played the role of Brij Nath in Mission Impossible – Ghost Protocol. Name this talented actor?

40) This director was born in Chennai and later went on to win two Filmfare awards for Best Director for the films 'Ghayal' and 'Damini'. Name this director?

41) This comedy movie directed by Bharat Rangachary was about a wealthy businesswoman wanting to marry a poor and honest man and her uncle was trying to find a suitable match for her. Name this movie?

42) He was born in Surat, Gujarat. Later he moved to Mumbai. His debut film was Hum Hindustani. He

went on to win 2 National Awards for Best Actor for Dastak and Koshish. Name this talented actor?

43) This film edited by Hrishikesh Mukherjee and directed by Rajinder Singh Bedi won 4 National Film Awards. Name this movie starring Sanjeev Kumar and Rehana Sultan?

44) This talented cinematographer won 5 National Awards for Cinematography. The last award was for the film Dharmatma (1976). Name this talented cinematographer?

45) Who played the role of Amarkant Varma an All India Radio Program Executive in the movie Dil Se?

46) Who won the National Award for Best Cinematography for the movie 'Dil Se'?

47) She was born in Shimla. She graduated in Criminal Psychology and won a Filmfare award for Best Debut in her first film. Name this talented actress?

48) This Bollywood romantic drama launched the careers of 2 leading actors and a playback singer. The movie has been rated as the top 25 Must See Bollywood Films by Indiatimes Movies. Name the film?

49) Who won the Star Screen Award for Best Male Playback for the song 'Chaiyya Chaiyya' from the movie Dil Se?

50) Who sang the iconic song 'Papa Kehte Hain' from the movie Qayamat Se Qayamat Tak?

51) This film based on the life of poet Mirza Ghalib directed by Sohrab Modi became the first film to win the National Award for Best Feature Film in Hindi. Who played the role of Mirza Ghalib in the film?

52) Bimal Roy won three National Awards for Best Feature Film in Hindi. Name the three films that got him the awards?

53) This film directed by B R Chopra won him his first National Award for Best Feature Film in Hindi. The film starred Rajendra Kumar, Ashok Kumar and Nanda. The film made a case against capital punishment. Name the film?

54) This film directed, acted and produced by Sunil Dutt won a National Award for Best Feature Film in Hindi for this film. Name the film?

55) This talented actor turned politician started his career in the Hindi service of Radio Ceylon. His debut film was Railway Platform. He got noticed in Mother India and never looked back after this iconic film. He won the Padma Shri in 1968. Name this actor?

56) Who played the role of Retired Major Chandrakant in the 1965 film 'Oonche Log' directed by Phani Majumdar?

57) This suspense thriller directed by B R Chopra went on to win the National Film Award for Best Feature Film in Hindi. The movie starred Sunil Dutt, Raaj Kumar and Mumtaz. Name the film?

58) This dancer and actress of Anglo-Burmese origin came to Mumbai from Burma in 1943 during World War 2. She got noticed with the song 'Mera Naam Chin Chin Chu' in the film 'Howrah Bridge'. She was recognized as the best item dancers in Hindi cinema. Name this actress cum dancer?

59) Who sang the song 'Zindagi Kaisi Hai Paheli' from the film 'Anand' by Hrishikesh Mukherjee?

60) Who won the National Film Award for Best Actor for the film 'Ardh Satya' directed by Govind Nihalini?

2.3 The New Millennium – this covers Hindi films made in the period 2000 onwards.

Questions –

1) What was the first Hindi movie to be shot in New Zealand?

2) He won the Filmfare Award for Best Male Playback singer. He has also sung the theme song of F1 Indian Grand Prix. Who is he?

3) Which Indian cricketer played a cameo role of a commentator in the movie 'Kai Po Che'?

4) Which veteran actor won the Dada Saheb Phalke award in 2012?

5) Who coached the women's hockey team for the movie 'Chak De! India'?

6) Who won the Best Supporting Actor award for the film Rock On?

7) Which film won the National Award for Best Popular Film Providing Wholesome Entertainment in 2007?

8) Who wrote the screen play for the films 'Khosla ka Ghosla' and 'Company'?

9) Name the well known singer who acted in the film 'Filhaal'?

10) What was Madhuri Dixit's comeback film in 2007?

11) Who won the National Film Awards for Best Actress for Mr and Mrs Iyer?

12) Mann is a copy of which English film?

13) What is the connection of Naina Lal Kidwai with the film 'Monsoon Wedding'?

14) Which Hindi film was awarded the Audience Award for Best Foreign Language Film at the 32nd Sao Paulo International Film Festival?

15) This film director was nominated for an Academy award and was a voting member for the Academy awards in 2005?

16) The following international cricketers played a cameo role in this movie – Allan Border, Ashish Nehra, Harbhajan Singh, and Martin Crowe. Name the film?

17) Tata Elxsi created the visual effects of this film set in the back drop of New York. Name the film?

18) Well known Bollywood music director, studied at Presidency College, Kolkata and FTII, Pune. His first break was composing the music for 'Mere Yar Ki Shaadi'. Who is he?

19) Who sung 'Main Aisa Kyun Hoon' from the film Lakshya?

20) Name the military academy showcased in the movie 'Lakshya'?

21) Which Hindi movie is inspired from the English movie 'An Affair to Remember'?

22) He started his career as an assistant direction in TV serials. He directed his first Bollywood film in 2003 which he quit during production. He was then diagnosed with leukaemia while filming 'Tumsa Nahin Dekha'. Name this Bollywood director?

23) This Bollywood composer was associated with a Bengali band 'Chandrabindoo'. He later moved to Mumbai after studying sound engineering at FTII, Pune. He went on to compose ad jingles before getting his break in films. Name this Bollywood composer?

24) He was born in Nagpur and studied film editing at FTII, Pune. He started work in films as an editor and creative producer. He went on to win National Film Awards in 2004, 2007 and 2010. Name this director?

25) Who played the role of Joy Lobo in the iconic film '3 Idiots'?

26) The Imperial College of Engineering shown in the film '3 Idiots' was shot in which institute?

27) Which Hindi movie is inspired from the English movie 'Memento'?

28) Who played the role of Bharat Bhusan in the comedy movie 'Bheja Fry'?

29) He started his career as an advertising professional and was into theatre as well. His first movie was 'Naseem'. His latest movie is Ankur Arora Murder case. Name the actor?

30) He plays rugby and is associated with numerous charities. He played the role of an investment banker in the film 'Chameli' and a military officer in the film 'Shaurya'. Name this talented actor?

31) This film by Rituparno Ghosh was an adaptation of the short story 'Gift of Magi' by O'Henry. The film went on to win the National Award for Best Hindi film. Name the film?

32) He won the Best Feature Film in Hindi with his debut directorial venture. He also won a Zee Cine Award for the Most Promising Director for the same film which featured Anupam Kher and Boman Irani. Name the director?

33) This iconic film went on to win 7 Filmfare Awards. The cast of the movie was featured on the September 2008 issue of Rolling Stone magazine in India. Name this movie?

34) She started acting with the movie 'Everybody Says I'm Fine'. She attended the Royal Academy of Dramatic Art. Name this talented actress cum anchor?

35) This film set in the background of Indo Pak war is about POW's in Pakistani jail who attempt to escape. The movie went on to win the National Award for Best Feature Film in Hindi. Name this movie?

36) This cult movie was rated by Rediff as among the Top 10 movies of the decade. It also won the National Film Award for Best Hindi Film. It was the directorial debut of a director turned actor who has left a mark in Hindi films. Name the film and the director?

37) Who played the role of Pooja is the hit movie 'Dil Chahta Hain'?

38) She has served as an assistant director in the films 'Lagaan', 'Monsoon Wedding'. She did her schooling in Kolkata and college in Mumbai. Name this director?

39) He is a versatile actor and director. He won the Best Feature Film in Hindi for Raghu Romeo as a director. He played the role of ISI chief in the film 'Agent Vinod'. Name this actor cum director?

40) She studied electrical engineering but went on to become a model. She acted in movies like 'Fashion', 'Dil Chahta Hain' and was also a VJ. Name this actress?

41) This film is a courtroom comedy and went on to win the National Award for Best Feature Film in Hindi. Saurabh Shukla also won the National Film Award for Best Supporting Actor for this film. Name the film?

42) This award winning film has 4 stories. It went on to win the National Film Award for Best Hindi Film and is also considered the first crowd-sourced from social networks Hindi film. Name the film?

43) Who played the role of Sukhdev in the movie 'Legend of Bhagat Singh'?

44) Who played the role of Suleiman Seth in the Shyam Benegal directed 'Zubeidaa'?

45) This movie about the relationship of a blind and deaf girl with her teacher draws inspiration from Helen Keller's life. This movie won the Filmfare award for Best Film. Name the film?

46) Sanjay Leela Bhansali has won two National Film Awards. Name the films for which we won the awards?

47) She won the Filmfare Award for Best Supporting Actress for Kuch Kuch Hota Hain. She later won the Filmfare Award for Best Actress for the movie Black. Name this talented actress?

48) Who played the role of Kusum Duggal in the film 'Do Dooni Chaar'?

49) For the movie 'Page 3' who won the Best Debut Female Award at the Zee Cine Awards?

50) Who played the role of Indira in the movie 'Paan Singh Tomar'?

51) She has acted in the Cadbury Diary Milk – Silk commercial. She made her film debut with a small role in an English film 'One Night with the King'. She won rave reviews for the film 'The Lunchbox'. Name this actress?

52) He won the National Film Award for Best Actor in 2012 for Paan Singh Tomar and Filmfare Critics Award for Best Actor for the same movie. Name this talented actor?

53) This actor passed out of National School of Drama. He went on win Filmfare Award for Best Supporting Actor for the film 'Lunchbox'. He also won a Screen Award for Best Supporting Actor for the film 'Talash'. Name this actor?

54) Who played the role of Roshni Shekhawat in the movie 'Talash'?

55) He played the role of a child actor in 'Yadon Ki Barat'. He went on to win the Filmfare Best Male Debut in 1989. He was later awarded a Padma Shri in 2003. Name this brilliant actor?

56) This film created awareness about dyslexic disorder in children. It went on to win the National Film Award for Best Film on Family Welfare. Name this film?

57) Aamir Khan played the role of Ram Shankar Nikumbh in Taare Zameen Par. Who was initially approached to play Nikumbh?

58) He is currently the chairperson of the Children Film's Society, India and has directed movies like 'Stanley

Ka Dabba' and 'Hawa Hawai'. Name this talented director?

59) Who played the role of Rosy Miss in the film 'Stanley Ka Dabba'?

60) This film by Vishal Bhardwaj won two National Film Awards and was nominated for 10 Filmfare Awards. Name this film?

61) He studied Economics at Deshbandhu College, Delhi. He gained recognition from the music he composed for Parineeta. He was also awarded the Filmfare R.D.Burman Award for New Music Talent in the same year. He later went on to win a National Film Award for Best Music Direction. Name this talented composer?

62) He has sung songs in Kannada, Hindi, Bengali and Marathi films. He won the Filmfare RD Burman Award for New Music Talent for the movie Murder. Name this well know singer?

63) Who played the role of Bikram Bose in Ali Abbas Zaffar directed 'Gunday'?

64) He was born in Jamshedpur. He studied at Hindu College, Delhi. He directed TV programs and later went into film direction. He directed films like 'Jab We Met', 'Love Aaj Kal'. Name this talented director?

65) He is son a former Nawab and Indian cricket captain. He has acted in films like 'Love Aaj Kal', 'Hum Tum'.He won the National Award for Best Actor for the film Hum Tum. Name this actor?

66) He is considered to be one of the finest actors in his generation. He has been nominated for CNN IBN Indian of the Year for the Entertainment Category

thrice. He won the Zee Cine Award for Best Actor Male for the film Barfi. Name this talented actor?

67) Who played the role of Naina Talwar, a nerdy topper in the film 'Yeh Jawani Hai Deewani' directed by Ayan Mukherjee?

68) He played the role of Rocky in Dilwale Dulhania Le Jayenge. Later went on to direct blockbuster hits like Kuch Kuch Hota Hain which won both Filmfare and National Awards. Name this talented director?

69) Karan Johar has won the Filmfare Award for Best Director for two of his films. Name these award wining films?

70) This VJ turned actor had a brief stint with Channel V before acting in films like London Dreams, Action Replay. He has won the IIFA Award for Best Supporting Actor for the film Yeh Jawani Hai Deewani. Name this actor?

71) Who played the role of Aisha Banerjee in the film 'Wake Up Sid' directed by Ayan Mukerji?

72) She started her career in television with Hum Panch. Her first film was Bhalo Theko in Bengali. Later she acted in numerous Hindi films starting with Parineeta which got her the Filmfare Award for Best Female Debut. She later won the National Film Award for Best Actress. Name this powerful actress?

73) He was born in Dubai. He studies Economics in Delhi and got admission to the Indian Institute of Management in Calcutta but could not complete the course as he wanted to pursue a career in films. His debut film was Miley Jab Hum Tum. Name this actor?

74) This film directed by Hansal Mehta starred Rajkummar Rao in a lead role. The story is about a

poor farmer from Rajasthan who comes to Mumbai for a better life. Name the film?

75) He graduated from the FTII Pune in 2008. His debut film was Love Sex and Dhoka. He recently won the National Film Award for Best Actor. Name this very talented young actor?

76) Who played the role of Master da Surya Sen in the historical war film 'Chittagong' directed by Bedabrata Pain?

77) He is one of the founder members of Theatre Action Group. He acted in films like Gandhi and Shatranj Ke Khiladi. He also played the role of Magistrate Wilkinson in the film 'Chittagong'. Name this theatre personality and actor?

78) City Lights directed by Hansal Mehta is a remake of which British Film that received a BAFTA nomination?

79) He made his debut with the film 'Maachis'. He has acted in films like Mere Yar Ki Shaadi, Munna Bhai, A Wednesday, My Name is Khan and Special 26. Name this actor?

80) She made her debut in the film Ishq Mein Jeena Ishq Mein Marna. She has won 2 IIFA Awards for Best Supporting Actress for the films Delhi 6 and Bhaag Milkha Bhaag. Name this talented actress?

81) He made his debut with the film 'Phool Aur Kante'. He has won 2 National Awards for Best Actor with the films 'Zakhm' and 'Legend of Bhagat Singh'. Name this talented actor?

82) This National Award winning film directed by Rituparno Ghosh is based on short story 'Gift of Magi'

by O'Henry and holds the record for completing shooting in 13 days. Name the film?

83) This film directed by Dibakar Banerjee won the National Film Award for Best Feature Film in Hindi. This was Dibakar's debut film and features Anupam Kher and Boman Irani. Name the film?

84) Who played the role of Kishen Khurana in the film 'Khosla Ka Ghosla' directed by Dibakar Banerjee?

85) This VJ turned actor made his debut with the film 'Ek Chhotisi Love Story'. He also went on to act in films like 'Lakshya'. "Traffic Signal' and 'Bheja Fry'. Name this talented actor?

86) This film directed by Amrit Sagar is based on the true story of prisoners of war from the 1971 Indo Pak War. The film went on to win the National Film Award for Best Feature Film in Hindi. Name the film?

87) This actor started with television and later moved to films. He won the National Award for Best Supporting Actor for Satya and later a Special Jury Award for Pinjar. Name this talented actor?

88) This director turned actor made his debut with the film 'Rock On' which went on to win 2 National Awards. He played the role of Aditya Shroff in the film. Name this director turned actor?

89) He started his career in television with the show 'Hip Hip Hooray'. He later became a VJ with Channel V. His debut film was 'Bus Yuhin'. He later acted in films like Supari, Woh Lamhe and Rock On. His role of KD in Rock On won him a Special Jury Certificate at the Filmfare Awards. Name the actor?

90) What disorder was Auro suffering from in the film 'Paa' directed by R Balki which won the National Award for Best Feature Film in Hindi?

91) Who played the role of Jagdish Tyagi aka Jolly in the National Award winning film 'Jolly LLB'?

92) This film directed by Sujoy Ghosh is a tribute to music legend R D Burman. The film starred Juhi Chawla, Sanjay Suri, Rahul Bose, Sayan Munshi, Rinkie Khanna and Riya Sen. Name the film?

93) This film directed by Onir and produced by Sanjay Suri went on to win the National Film Award for Best Feature Film in Hindi. Sanjay Suri also acted in this film. Name the film?

94) This cult film was centered on the life of 3 friends and how their relationship evolves over time. It won debutant director Farhan Akthar the National Film Award for Best Feature Film in Hindi. Name the film?

95) Who won the National Award for Best Male Playback Singer for the song 'Jaane Kyon' from the film 'Dil Chahta Hai'?

96) This film directed by Rajat Kapoor went on to win the National Film Award for Best Feature Film in Hindi. The film starred Vijay Raaz and Saurabh Shukla. Name the film?

97) This film is based on Chetan Bhagat's novel '3 Mistakes of My Life'. The film was directed by Abhishek Kapoor and met with box office success. Name the film?

98) Who played the role of Arjun Harishchand Waghmare in the film 'Hawa Hawaai'?

99) What is common to the films 'Dil Chahta Hai', 'Lakshya', 'Rock On' and 'Luck by Chance'?

100) This alumnus of FTII, Pune started his career as an assistant to Vidhu Vinod Chopra and later went on to direct films like 'Khamoshi', 'Devdas', 'Black'. Name the director?

Chapter Three – Bengali Movies Quiz

3   Bengali Movies Quiz

Bengali Cinema had a humble beginning with bioscopes shown in well known theatres at the close of the 19th century. The first Bengali movie to be made was 'Billamangal' by Hiralal Sen. Hiralal Sen was one of the pioneers of Bengali cinema and directed silent films. The first Bengali talkie to be made was 'Jamai Shasthi' released in 1931. The early heroes were Pramathesh Barua and Debaki Bose. In the 1950's and 1960's considered the 'Golden Period' of commercial Bengali cinema emerged super starts like Uttam Kumar and Suchitra Sen. Their pairing in numerous films has immortalized them as the first romantic 'Bengali couple' in cinema. Bengali cinema went on to produce numerous directors of international repute like Satyajit Ray, Mrinal Sen and Ritwik Ghatak in the 1960's.

They won numerous awards at National Film Awards and International Film Festivals with their parallel cinema. Till date Satyajit Ray holds the record with 7 Best Director Awards at the National Film Awards. Numerous directors of national repute like Bimal Roy, Rituparno Ghosh, Tapan Majumdar, Tapan Sinha, Buddhadeb Dasgupta, Aparna Sen, Sandip Ray and Goutam Ghosh have left their imprints on Bengali cinema with their great work. In recent years there have been a new generation of Bengali directors like Srijit Mukherji, Aniruddha Roy Choudhury, Kaushik Ganguly, Mainak Bhaumik, Anik Dutta, and Anjan Dutta who have made interesting films who continue the rich tradition of Bengali cinema being different and unique as well as enriching. It is also interesting to note that Bengali cinema has used the richness of Bengali literature to come up with a unique brand of cinema. Bengali detective movies are an example of this trend where Bengali detective novels have found a new life in wider audiences due to the popularity gained from movies. Feluda and Byomkesh stories are available in English making it accessible to a wider audience.

Byomkesh Bakshi has already been adopted in Hindi serials on National television and now Dibakar Banerjee is about to make a series of Byomkesh Bakshi movies. This has also resulted in a renewed interest in reading the detective novels of Byomkesh and Feluda, immortalizing these sleuths for future generations to come as well. Lot of the original stories have now been translated into English and other Indian languages.

Questions –

1) What was the first silent Bengali movie?

2) Which Bengali film won the award of Best Human Document at the 1956 Cannes Film Festival?

3) Who were known as the Eternal Pair of Bengali Cinema?

4) Who was the first Bengali director to win the Russian Order of Friendship?

5) Name the national level bodybuilder featured in Ray's classic 'Joy Baba Felunath'?

6) Who played the role of Nar Singh in the film Abhijan directed by Satyajit Ray?

7) Which Bengali movie is inspired by the novel 'Prisoner of Zenda' by Anthony Hope?

8) Who played the role of Sister Nivedita in the Bhagini Nivedita?

9) About which actor did Satyajit Ray remark 'had Mr.Chakraborty been born in the US, he would have been awarded an Oscar for his acting'?

10) This 1971 film won the National Film Award for Best Feature Film and featured the life of a sales manager in a British fan company.

11) What was the name of Uttam Kumar's first feature film? This was never released.

12) Which English movie was influenced by the 1962 Satyajit Ray classic 'Abhijaan'?

13) Who played the character Gulabi in the movie 'Abhijaan'?

14) Who composed music for Mrinal Sen's film Akash Kusum released in 1965?

15) Who won the Filmfare Awards East for Best Male Actor (Critics) in 2014?

16) Which renowned Bengali actor made his debut in the film 'Annapurnar Mandir' in 1936?

17) Who played the role of sleuth Byomkesh Bakshi in the film 'Shajarur Kanta'?

18) Who played the role of Pritish Sarkar in Ray's classic 'Nayak'?

19) Which Bengali film received the 1975 award for Best Film for Children and Young adults in Tehran?

20) The Hindi movie 'Bawarchi' was adopted from which Bengali movie directed by Tapan Sinha?

21) Which Bengali actor has the distinction of having been offered the roles of Feluda as well as Byomkesh Bakshi?

22) Who played the role of Tarini Khuro in Sandip Ray's 'Jekhane Bhuter Bhoy'?

23) This iconic Bengali film was nominated for the Golden Bear at the 20th Berlin Film Festival. It is based on a novel by Sunil Gangopadhyay with the same name as the film. Name the film?

24) This director won the National Film Award's Rajat Kamal Award for Best Story in 1974 for Jukti Takko Aar Gappo. Name this eminent director?

25) Who won the National Film Award for Best Actress for the film 'Dibratir Kabya'?

26) What is Abir Chatterjee's first Feluda film directed by Sandip Ray?

27) Who played the role of Sujata Mitra in "Chowringhee (1968)?

28) Who played the role of Nita in Ritwik Ghatak's 'Meghe Dhaka Tara (1960)'?

29) This firm featured the life of a foley artist and went on to win the National Film Award for Best Bengali Film?

30) Ritwik Chakraborty played the role of 'Tarak' a foley artist in Kaushik Ganguly's 'Shabdo'. Who was originally considered for the role of Tarak?

31) This award winning director studied Economics at Presidency College and dabbled in theatre before venturing into films. He has been a lyricist for movies like 'Cross Connection' and 'Madly Bangalee'. Name the director?

32) He acted as Shyamal in Ray's 'Seemabaddha'. An advertising professional and author, he also acted in theatre playing the role of Feluda in Feluda Pherot a play by Srijit Mukherjee. Name the actor?

33) This iconic actress refused the Dada Saheb Phalke Award in 2005 and is known as the 'Greta Garbo of India'. Name the actress?

34) This film by Satyajit Ray won the National Award for Best Film in 1965 and won Ray his second Silver Bear for Best Director at the Berlin Film Festival. This film is based on 'Nostonir' a novel by Rabindranath Tagore. Name the film?

35) This film won the Certificate of Merit for 3rd Best Bengali Film at the National Film Awards and is inspired by the Hollywood flick 'Random Harvest'. Name the film?

36) The film Jalsaghar was shot in which location?

37) Who directed the classic Uttam Kumar, Suchitra Sen starrer 'Saptapadi' that also won the Certificate of Merit for Second Best Feature Film in Bengali?

38) This film directed by Mrinal Sen went on to win a National Film Award. It was also the debut film of actor Subhendu Chatterjee. Name the film?

39) Sonar Kella (Golden Fortress directed by Satyajit Ray won the National Award for Best Screenplay, Direction and also won the National Award for Best Child Artist. Name the child actor who won this award?

40) Who directed the movie Kabuliwala which went on to win the National Award for Best Film and Best Bengali Film in the same year?

41) What was Dr.Hajra's profession in the movie Sonar Kella?

42) This movie featured the life of a foley artist and went on to win the National Film Award for Best Bengali film. Name this film?

43) Who played the role of Paromita in Aparna Sen's National Award winning film 'Paromitar Ek Din'?

44) This talented director has acted in films like Dutta vs. Dutta, Shabdo. Written lyrics for Cross Connection and has also dabbled in theatre before venturing into films. Name the director?

45) She studied at Lady Brabourne College and made her debut with Aparna Sen's 'Swet Patharer Thala'. She went on to win the National Award for Best Actress in the movie 'Dahan'. Name this talented actress?

46) Who played the role of Sadat Manto in Srijit Mukherjee directed 'Mishawr Rahashyo'?

47) This film directed by Kamaleshwar Mukherjee won the Centenary Award at the International Film Festival of India, Goa 2013 and dealt with the life of eccentric film maker Ritwik Ghatak. Name this film?

48) This film explores the relationship of a retired man and a 5 year old girl. It went on the win the National Award for Best Feature Film in Bengali. Name the film?

49) He studied Economics at Presidency College. His first film 'Podokkhep' won him the National Award for Best Feature Film in Bengali. Name this talented director?

50) He has directed two National Award winning films. He started his career with advertisements for Philips, Britannia. Name this director?

51) His maternal grandfather was Ritwik Ghatak. His debut film as an actor was Sandip Ray's 'Bombaiyer Bombete'. He later went on to direct films. Name this talented actor and director?

52) Who was the music director for the film 'Hawa Bodol'?

53) He studied at Goenka College of Commerce and at ICFAI Business School. His debut movie was Cross Connection. He played the role of Doctor S P Mukherjee in 'Meghe Dhaka Tara'. Name this talented actor?

54) Who played the role of Piya in the comedy film 'Cross Connection'?

55) A recipient of a National Film Award for Best Male Playback Singer. He studied at Ashutosh College and later went on to start a famous Bangla band. He sang the song 'Who Am I' from the film 'Bedroom'. Name this talented singer?

56) She has won a National Film Award for Best Female Playback Singer. She also won the Children's special episode of 'Sa Re Ga Ma'. She sang the song 'Arekta Din' from the Bengali movie Bedroom. Name this talented singer?

57) This comedy film directed by Parambrata Chatterjee is inspired by the English movie 'The Change-Up'. Name the film?

58) He studied medicine at Kolkata Medical College and later become a well known actor in Bengali films. He made his debut in Mrinal Sen's Akash Kusum. Name this talented actor?

59) Who played the role of an air hostess, Sujata Mitra in the 1968 film Chowringhee?

60) He was born in Jamshedpur. He starred opposite Jaya Bhaduri in the film Guddi. He also played the role of Hari in the film 'Aranyer Din Ratri'. Name this actor?

61) This film directed by Goutam Ghosh highlighted the problem of tribal interests being ignored for commercial interests in bauxite mining in the backdrop of Maoist problems. The film starred Soumitra Chatterjee, Konkona Sen Sharma and Priyanshu Chatterjee. Name the film?

62) Who played the role of Jhilik Bose in the film Shunyo Awnko by Gautam Ghosh?

63) He was born in Delhi. He has acted in both Hindi and Bengali films. His debut film was Tum Bin. He also played the role of Jyotirindranath Tagore in the film 'Moner Manush'. Name the actor?

64) Her debut film was Hemanter Pakhi. She has acted in numerous other films like Take One, Jaatishwar. Name this actress?

65) He studied at Scottish Church College in Kolkata. He has acted in Bengali theatre and films. His recent work includes Dutta vs. Dutta and Roopkatha Noy. Name this talented actor?

66) She was crowned Miss India Earth in 2002. She studied from Carmel Convent School in Kolkata. She has acted in serials like Buddha, Karam Apnaa Apnaa. She also acted in the Bengali film 'Aborto'. Name this actress?

67) Who played the role of Feluda in the Sandip Ray directed film 'Kailashey Kelenkari'?

68) This talented actress was born in Comilla district in Bangladesh. She has been awarded the Padma Shri. She has acted in numerous films with Uttam Kumar

like 'Dhanni Meye', 'Haat Baraley Bandhu'. Name this talented actress?

69) He started his career with a small role in Satyajit Ray's Seemabaddha. He also acted in Ganashatru and Aguntuk. He won a National Film Award for Best Supporting Actor for the film Parama. Name this actor?

70) This well known National Award winning director also has acted in many films. He played the role of Anando in Chalo Let's Go. Name this talented actor and director?

71) This satirical film about the future of ghosts became one of biggest hits in Bengali cinema in recent times. It has also been remade in Hindi. Name the film?

72) Who played the role of Darpa Narayan Chowdhury in the film 'Bhooter Bhabishyat' directed by Anik Dutta?

73) This actor turned politician was born in Tezpur, Assam. He later went on to act in both Bengali and Assamese films. He played the role of Mr. Ramsey in Bhooter Bhabishyat. Name this actor turned politician?

74) She has acted in both Bengali television and films. Her recent films include Chaar, Nirbhoya and Aschorjo Prodip. She was nomination for a Filmfare Award for Best Actor Supporting Role (Female) – Bengali for the movie Aschorjo Prodip. Name the actress?

75) Who played the role of Papu Bhai in the film Damadol?

76) Who is scheduled to play the role of Topshe in the upcoming Feluda film 'Badshahi Angti' directed by Sandip Ray?

77) This actor has dabbled in theatre, television and films. He played the role of Prodip Dutta in the movie Aschorjo Prodip. Name this talented actor?

78) Who composed the music for Mainak Bhaumik directed 'Maach Misti and More'?

79) He has edited movies like Bong Connection and Chalo Let's Go. His directorial debut was the film Aamra. His next directorial venture was Bedroom. Name this talented director?

80) This thriller film directed by Aniruddha Roy Chowdhury is based on a novel by Samaresh Majumdar of the same name. The film deals with the underworld smuggling business. Name the film?

81) This movie was director Srijit Mukherji's debut film and it was a tribute to Satyajit Ray's classic film 'Nayak'. Name the film?

82) She is the daughter of a renowned economist and played the role of Srinandita in the film 'Autograph' directed by Srijit Mukherjee?

83) This director played the role of Abhiroop Sen in the film 'Arekti Premer Golpo' directed by Kaushik Ganguly. Name the director who acted in this film?

84) This film directed by Goutam Ghosh is based on the life of Lalan Fakir. It went on to win the National Film Award for Best Feature Film on National Integration. Name the film?

85) Who played the role of Jyotirindranath Tagore in the film 'Moner Manush' directed by Goutam Ghosh?

86) He is one of leading actors in Bengali cinema and won the National Film Award – Special Jury Award

for his role in the film 'Dosar'. Name this talented actor?

87) This film is based on a novel of the same name by Satyajit Ray. It was actor Bibhu Bhattacharya's last film as he passed away after the dubbing. Name the film?

88) This film directed by Aparna Sen also features her daughter Konkona Sen Sharma and they both play the same character. Aparna Sen went on to win the Best Director Award for this film at the New York Indian Film Festival. Name the film?

89) Who played the role of Satyabati in 'Abar Byomkesh' directed by Anjan Dutta?

90) Who sang the song 'Jawl Phoring' from the movie 'Hemlock Society?

91) He studied engineering at Jadavpur University and worked at Texas Instruments before becoming a music composer. His debut film was 'Autograph'. He has won the Star Anand Sera Bangali Award in the music category. Name this talented composer?

92) He won his first National Film Award for Best Male Playback Singer for the movie 'Jaatishwar'. Name this talented singer?

93) She won the Best Actress Award at the Madrid International Film Festival for the film 'Jara Bristite Bhijechhilo'. She has also won a National Film Award for Best Actress for the film 'Dahan'. Name this talented actress?

94) He made his debut in Mrinal Sen's 'Interview'. He later went on to become one of the leading romantic heroes of 1970's. Name this actor?

95) Who played the role of Andy a budding musician in the film 'Bong Connection'?

96) This Bengali film directed by Tapan Sinha stars Dilip Kumar and Saira Banu. The film is based on the labour movement in the early 1940's. Name the film?

97) He has been a playback singer in both Bengali and Hindi films. He was won numerous Bengali Film Journalist's Association Awards for film like Goopy Bagha Phire Elo and Sagina Mahato. Name this talented singer?

98) This film is set in the background of the Naxal movement in West Bengal and features the story of young man trying to find a job in trying circumstances. Dhritiman Chatterjee played the lead role. Name this film?

99) Who played the role of Goopy and Bagha in Satyajit Ray's classic 'Hirak Rajar Deshe'?

100)This Bengali film directed by Goutam Halder won the National Film Award for Best Cinematography and Best Audiography. This was also Vidya Balan's debut film. Name the film?

101)'Joy Baba Felunath' was shot in Varanasi and Kolkata. Which palace of a former Raja served as the hideout for Macchli Baba?

102)The war scene in 'Goopy Gyne Bagha Byne' was shot in Jaisalmer and involved 1000 camels. Who supplied the camels to the film unit?

103)Who played the double role of King of Shundi and King of Halla in 'Goopy Gyne Bagha Byne?

104)He has played the role of Topshe in Ray's films 'Sonar Kella' and 'Joy Baba Felunath'. He later became an entrepreneur and is a co-founder of the restaurant chain 'Bhojohari Manna'. Name this actor turned businessman?

105)Who played the role of Pritish Sarkar an advertising executive in the film 'Nayak'?

106)What is common to these films directed by Mrinal Sen, 'Bhuvan Shome', 'Ek Din Pratidin' and 'Akaler Sandhane'?

107)This film featuring Soumitra Chatterjee, Aparna Sen and Subhendu Chatterjee was about a young middle class executive who tries to rise in stature for greater social acceptance and bluffs a young girl. Name the film?

108)Who played the role of Anjan Sen in Mrinal Sen's award wining film 'Kharij'?

109)This film directed by Anjan Dutta is based on a Bengali rock band that rehearses in a garage in Kolkata. Name the film?

110)This film directed by Tapan Sinha and set in the backdrop of political violence in Bengal went on to win a National Film Award for Best Feature Film in Bengali. It was later made into a Hindi film 'Mere Apne'. Name the film?

Chapter Four – Regional Movies Quiz

4   Regional Movies Quiz

Regional movies have a rich history in India. This chapter has questions from a wide range of regional films including Tamil, Malayalam, Telegu, Kannada, Assamese, Oriya, Gujarati and Marathi films. Tamil films started with the first silent talkie 'Keechaka Vadham' in 1916. The first Tamil talkie was Kalidas released in 1931. Today Tamil film industry is booming and one of the largest film producers in the country. Tamil films are also made in Sri Lanka, Malaysia, Singapore and Canada where there is a significant Tamil diaspora.

Telegu Cinema is also known as Tollywood. R.V.Naidu is considered the father of Telegu cinema and produced the first silent Telegu film 'Bhisma Pratigna' in 1921. Telegu film industry ranks second in India in terms of films produced annually.

Malayalam films kicked off in the 1920's and were initially based in Trivandrum. Later Chennai became the hub of Malayalam films in the 1940's and again moved back to Kerala in 1980's. The world first film with a single actor was made in 2001 (The Guard).

Kannada film industry is based in Bangalore and produces more than 100 films each year. The first film made in Kannada was Sati Sulochana in 1934. Gubbi Veeranna was considered the doyen of Kannada cinema in the 1940's. The rise of Rajkumar in the 1950's resulted in a new direction in Kannada films towards historical epic films.

Assamese films started in 1935 with Jyoti Prasad Agarwala making 'Joymati'. Assamese films are characterized by a slow pace and sensitive portrayal of subjects. The leading directors have been Bhabendra Nath Saikia and Jahnu Barua.

Oriya film industry is based in Cuttack. There was no silent film era for Oriya films. The first talkie 'Sita Bibaha' was made in 1936 by Mohan Sundar Deb Goswami. Oriya film industry has grown slowly over time. It has produced some fine actors like Uttam Mohanty, Bijay Mohanty, Prasanta Nanda and Nandita Das. Some Bengali directors like Mrinal Sen have made Oriya films.

Gujarati cinema started in the 1932 with the release of Narsinh Mehta the first Gujarati film. Bhavni Bhavai (1980) directed by Ketan Mehta was one of the few films to win National Film Awards. Gujarati cinema has gone on a decline over the years. Recently 'The Good Road' became the first Gujarati film to be selected to represent India in the Oscars in 2013.

Marathi film industry dates back to 1912 when the first silent movie Shree Pundalik was released. This was followed by Raja Harishchandra. Ayodhyecha Raja was the first talkie released in 1932. The great directors include V.Shantaram, Bhalji Pendharkar, Dada Konde and others. Harishchandrachi Factory released in 2009 depicted the struggle Dadasaheb went through in making Raja Harishchandra.

Questions –

1) Who directed the first Tamil silent movie 'Keechaka Vadham' in 1916?

2) Which was the first talkie film in Tamil?

3) Which Tamil movie starring M.G.Ramachandran was the first movie to get an adult certificate from the censor board?

4) Which Tamil movie was included in Time magazine's 'All Time 100 Best Movies' list?

5) This epic Tamil movie made in the late 1940's, became a nationwide hit and went on to be translated into English, Japanese and Danish. Name the movie?

6) This actor was called the 'Marlon Brando of Indian Cinema'. He also became the first Indian actor to win 'Best Actor' award at the Afro Asian Film Festival held in Egypt in 1960. Name the actor?

7) Kamal Haasan acted in the film 'Manmadha Leelai'. Who directed this movie?

8) This eminent director has won the Dada Saheb Phalke Award and has served as the director of the FTII Pune. He directed a documentary called 'Romance of Rubber'. Name the director?

9) An actress who has won the National Award for Best Actress as well as National Film Award for Best Costume design. Who is she?

10) Name the first Oriya talkie?

11) Name the first Oriya film to win the National Award?

12) This Oriya film was directed by Mrinal Sen and went on to fetch a National Award for Best Actor awarded to Prashanta Nanda?

13) Who won the National Award for Best actor for the film 'Nua Bou'?

14) This film was screened at the Cannes Film Festival and went on to win the Grand Prix award at Sochi International Film Festival, Russia in 1995. The film also won a special jury award at the National Film Awards in 1994. Name the film?

15) This award winning actress has acted in Oriya, Hindi, Bengali, Malayalam and Telegu films. She was the

first Indian woman to be inducted into the International Women's Forum hall of fame. Who is she?

16) Name the Oriya film that won the National Award for Best Oriya film in 2008?

17) Name the first 3D film made in India?

18) This Malayalam film is considered the world's first film to feature a single actor. Name this film?

19) This 1997 film was the first Malayalam film to represent India as the Best Foreign Language Film category at the Academy Awards?

20) Elippathayam (1981) was the first Malayalam film to win the British Film Institute Award. Who directed this movie?

21) This film on Formula 2 racing was abandoned. It featured Mohanlal as a racing driver. Name the film?

22) Who acted as the lead star in Priyadarshan's 'Kalapani' set in the background of Cellular Jail in Port Blair?

23) This award winning Malayali actor won the National Award 3 times and acted as a district collector in 'The King'. Name the actor?

24) This well known Bollywood actress acted with Mohanlal and Mammooty in the Malayali film 'The Harikrishnans'. Name the actress?

25) This movie directed by Shaji N Karun went on to win the National Film Award for Best Feature Film in 1989. It also won awards at Edinburgh International Film Festival as well as the Cannes Film Festival. Name the film?

26) This Assamese film directed by Brajen Barua went on to win the National Film Award for Best Assamese Film. Later a Hindi film 'Shivam' was made based on this film. Name this film?

27) This Assamese film featured a love story between a British tea estate owner and local tea garden worker. It won the National Award for Best Assamese Film. Name this film?

28) Which regional film industry is better known as 'Jollywood'?

29) Which was the first Assamese film in 1935?

30) This award wining Assamese director won the National Award for Best Assamese film for Ajeyo. He has also made a Hindi film 'Maine Gandhi Ko Nahi Mara'. Name this director?

31) This was the first Assamese film to be produced by National Film Development Corporation of India. It was also the first film directed by Jahnu Barua. Name this film?

32) This film directed by Bhabendra Nath Saikia involved a wealthy businessman who opts for a second marriage. This film went on to win the National Award - Rajat Kamal for best regional film in 1985. Name this film?

33) This well known actor of Assamese films was born in Dibrugarh. His first film was Dr.Bezbaruah. He has also acted in Bengali movies. Name this actor?

34) This talented actress was the first Assamese actress to win the National Film Award for Best Actress for the Assamese film 'Firingoti'. Her debut film was 'Agnisnan'. Name this actress?

35) This Assamese film went on to win 2 National Awards – for Second Best Feature Film and Best Actress. It was directed by Jahnu Barua and the story was set in 1962. Name this film?

36) This film directed by Padum Baruah was based on a novel of the same name by Dr.Laxminandan Borah. Name this film?

37) This film is about 4 unemployed youths from Tinsukia. Zubin Garg composed the music of this film and also acted in it. The film was shortlisted for the Indian Panorama. Name this film?

38) This film deals with the human-elephant conflict in Assam. Directed by Hiren Bora, it went on to win the National Film Award for Best Assamese Film. Name this film?

39) Which regional film industry in India is better known as 'Chandanavana' or 'Sandalwood'?

40) This iconic star of Kannada film industry acted in over 200 films. He won the Dada Saheb Phalke Award. He was kidnapped by the forest brigand Veerappan and was release after 108 days. Name this star?

41) This talented actor – director had an untimely end in a car accident. He is best known for Malgudi Days. He won a National Film Award for Best Film on Other Social Issues for his film 'Accident'. Name this talented actor- director?

42) This film directed by Rajendra Singh Babu starred Vishnuvardhan and Suhasini. The story was about a doctor who falls in love with his student. Name this film?

43) This film directed by Dinesh Babu won accolades at the Karnataka State Film Awards. It starred Vishnuvardhan in the role of an architect. Name this film?

44) This film written and directed by B.A.Arasu Kumar and went on win the National Film Award for Best Feature Film in Kannada. The film starred Rajkumar and Kalpana. Name this film?

45) This film directed by Shankar Nag won the Second Best Film Award as well as the Best Actor Award at the Karnataka State Film Awards 1980. Anant Nag won the Best Actor award for this film. Name the film?

46) This film is based on the novel 'Financial Expert' by RK Narayan. This film went on the win the National Award for Best Kannada film in 1984. Name the film?

47) Who won the best actor award at the Karnataka State Film Awards in 1984 for Banker Margayya?

48) This film won Karnataka State Film Awards for Best Film, Best Actor, Best Music Director and Best Dialogue Writer. Rajkumar the renowned actor also won the National Film Award for Best Male Playback Singer for the same film. Name this film?

49) He is the son of a famous Kannada actor. He won the Filmfare Award for Best Actor – Kannada for the film 'Om'. He also won the Karnataka State Film Award for Best Actor for the same film. Name this actor?

50) This theatre and film actor was best known for his portrayal of Sandalwood brigand Veerappan. He went on to win the Karnataka State Film Award for Best Actor for the film 'Veerappan'. Name the actor?

51) He was a gold medallist from the Film and Television Institute. He has won the National Film Award for Best Feature films four times. His first National Award was for the film 'Ghatashradda'. Name this talented director?

52) This film directed by Indrajit Lankesh went on to win the Karnataka State Film Award for Best Film in 2004. Name the film?

53) This well known director of Marathi films went on to win the Dada Saheb Phalke Award. He directed films like 'Bajirao Mastani', 'Rani Rupmati'. Name the director?

54) Who founded the Maharashtra Film Company in 1919?

55) This Marathi film won the President's Gold Medal at the first National Film Awards in 1954. Name the film?

56) This film was the first Indian and Marathi film to win the Best Film Award at the Venice film festival in 1937. Name the film?

57) This well known Marathi actor and director entered the Guinness Book of World Records for the highest number of films that achieved a silver jubilee. Name this personality?

58) This film directed by Sandeep Sawant, was the 2nd Marathi Film to win the National Film Award for Best Film. It was also India's official entry to the Oscars for Best Foreign Film in 2004.

59) He was the music director for the National Award winning Marathi film 'Shwaas'. He also won the National Film Award for Music direction for the film 'Chaitra'. Name this well known music composer?

60) Who won the National Film Award for Best Child Artist for the Marathi film 'Shwaas'?

61) Who was known as the Father of Telegu cinema?

62) This film was the first Telegu film to be premiered at the India International Film Festival in Mumbai in 1952. This film starred NT Rama Rao, S.V.Ranga Rao and Girija. Name the film?

63) Name the first Telegu film of the silent era?

64) The first Telegu talkie was produced by HM Reddy and was released in 1932. Name the film?

65) This film directed by K Raghavendra Rao and starring Chiranjeevi became the first Telegu film to gross over 10 Crore at the box office. Name the film?

66) Which film is considered to be the highest grossing Telegu film of all time?

67) This film went on to win the National Film Award for Best Telegu Film in 1986. The film starred Kamal Haasan and Raadhika. Name the film?

68) This musical drama film directed by K Vishwanath won 4 National Awards including National Award for Best Popular Film Providing Wholesome Entertainment. The film was premiered at the Moscow Film Festival in 1980. Name the film?

69) Who won the National Film Award for Best Male Playback Singer for the film Sankarabharanam in 1980?

70) Which was the first Gujarati movie to be released in India?

71) Who played the role of Maharaja Dhiraj Chandrasen in the Gujarati film 'Bhavni Bhavai' directed by Ketan Mehta?

72) This Gujarati film directed by Ketan Mehta went on to win 2 National Awards for National Integration and Best Art Direction in 1980. Name the film?

73) Nirupa Roy, the renowned actress of yesteryears made her debut in this Gujarati film made in 1948 directed by R H Punater. Name the film?

74) This film featured Bollywood actress Asha Parekh and was her first Gujarati film. It was released in 1963 and became a huge hit. Name the film?

75) This early 80's film made by Arun Bhatt received the Best Film Award from the Government of Gujarat. Name the film?

76) This Tamil drama film starred Prakash Raj and Shriya Reddy. This film directed by Priyadarshan went on to win National Award for Best Feature Film and Best Actor. Name the film?

77) This Tamil film made in 1937 is considered to be South India's first children's film. Name the film?

78) Which child artist in Tamil cinema came to be known as 'Shirley Temple of India'?

79) This was the second Tamil film to be dubbed into Japanese. This musical drama film featured Rajnikanth. Name the film?

80) This film directed by Ameer Sultan was shot in and near Madurai. It went on to win 2 National Awards for Best Actress and Best Editing in 2007. Name the movie?

81) She has won 3 Best Actress Awards at the Tamil Nadu State Film Awards and has won a Filmfare Award for Best Actress for the film Kushi. Name this talented actress?

82) He has won 4 National Film Awards and 10 Tamil Nadu State Film Awards. Some of his notable films include Nayagan, Hey Ram, and Dasavathaaram. Name this talented actor?

83) He is considered one of the great directors in Indian cinema. He was won 6 National Film Awards. His film 'Nayagan' was named in Time Magazine's list of 100 All Time Great Movies. Name this director?

84) This Oriya film set in the background of the 1999 super cyclone that hit Orissa causing immense damage. The film went on to win the National Film Award for Best Feature Film in Oriya. Name the film?

85) This film won the Filmfare Award East for Best Film in Assamese in 2013. It is set in the backdrop of Assam agitation and its aftermath. Kapil Bora won the Filmfare Award for Best Actor Male – Assamese for this film. Name the film?

86) She made her debut as a child actor in the Assamese film 'Abhimaan' in 1990. She is the first Assamese heroine to start a production house. She recently won the Filmfare Award East for Best Actress – Assamese for the film 'Dwaar'.Name this talented actress?

87) He has won the Odisha Living Legend Award in 2012. He has acted in over 130 Oriya films and 30 Bengali films. Name this talented actor of Oriya Cinema?

88) This film set in the background of Chilka Lake and its fishing community and their exploitation in the hands of fishing companies. This film went on to win the

National Film Award for Best Oriya film in 1978. Name the film?

89) This Marathi film set in the background of women representation in politics and political games went on to win the National Film Award for Best Marathi Film in 1999. Name the film?

90) This Marathi film is inspired by the Hollywood film 'Falling Down' starring Michael Douglas. The film was directed by Nishikant Kamat and went on to win the National Film Award for Best Marathi Film in 2005?

Chapter Five - Indian Movies at Film Festivals Quiz

5   Indian Movies at Film Festivals

Indian films have been screened at International Film Festivals since pre-independence days. One of the first films that got noticed and recognized at Cannes was Chetan Anand's 'Neecha Nagar' in 1946. This film was based on a novel by Hyatulla Ansari and went on to win the Grand Prix for International Film that year. Indian films have also been screened at other international festivals like Berlin, Moscow, Venice etc. Indian films have also been awarded at the British Academy of Film and Television Arts (BAFTA) and also at the Oscars. Some great Indian directors to be awarded at these festivals and BAFTA include Chetan Anand, Bimal Roy, V.Shantaram, Satyajit Ray, Mrinal Sen, Mira Nair, Adoor Gopalakrishnan and Sanjay Leela Bhansali. With Indian cinema now being marketed through digital channels, there is now a profusion of Indian cinema being shown at film festivals like Indian Film Festival of Los Angeles, Indian Film Festival of Melbourne and others.

Now time to put on the quizzing hats!

Questions –

1) Name the only Indian actress to win a BAFTA award?

2) Name the first Indian film to be awarded the BAFTA award for Best Film from any source?

3) Satyajit Ray went on to win 3 BAFTA awards for Best Film from any source. The first was for Pather Panchali. Name the other two films which were awarded the Best Film?

4) This Marathi movie directed by V Shantaram went on to be nominated for Grand Prix prize at Cannes Film

Festival. It however won an award for sound recording. Name the film?

5) This Bimal Roy classic went on to win the International Prize at the Cannes Film festival and was the 2nd Indian film after Neecha Nagar (1946) to win this prize. Name the film?

6) This movie by Mrinal Sen was nominated for the Golden Palm at the Cannes Film Festival and went on to win the Jury Prize at the same festival in 1983. Name the movie?

7) This singer-actor turned director won the best newcomer actor for Mrinal Sen's 'Chalochitra' at the Venice Film Festival. Name the actor?

8) Mrinal Sen won the Silver Prize for this film at the Moscow International Film Festival in 1975. He also won a National Award for the same movie. Name the movie?

9) This National Award winning director has also served as Jury at the Moscow International Film Festival in 1981. Name the director?

10) Akaler Sandhane directed by Mrinal Sen was nominated for Golden Bear at the Berlin International Film Festival in 1981. What award did the film win?

11) This film directed by Mrinal Sen went on to win him the Best Director award at the Cairo International Film Festival. The leading lady Nandita Das also won the Best Actress Award at the same festival. Name this film?

12) This film by Tapan Sinha won him the Best Film Award at the Asia Pacific Film Festival. The lead actor, Ashok Kumar was also nominated for Best Actor at the National Film Awards. Name the film?

13) Alumnus of National School of Drama, this actor has acted in movies, television and plays. He is the recipient of Silver Peacock, IFFI in 1987 and Critics Award, Venice Film Festival in 1986. He never won a National Award. Name this talented actor?

14) This film directed by an award wining director was nominated for the Golden Bear at the Berlin Film Festival in 1988. This film also won the National Film Award for Best Screenplay. Name the film?

15) This film by Buddhadeb Dasgupta was nominated for the Golden Lion at the Venice Film Festival in 2000 and went on to win the Special Director Award at the same festival. Name the film?

16) This award winning director was awarded the Dada Saheb Phalke Award in 2004. He has also won the prestigious Legion of Honour and British Film Institute Award. Name this director?

17) This award winning director won Silver Bear for Best Director at the Berlin Film Festival in 1964 and 1965. He is the only Indian director till date to win this award. Name this iconic director?

18) This film directed by Mrinal Sen went on to be nominated for the Golden Prize at Moscow International Film Festival and also won a National Award for Best Film in 1976. Name the film?

19) This film directed by Adoor Gopalakrishnan won a National Award and was also nominated for the Golden Prize at the Moscow International Film Festival in 1973. Name the film?

20) This film directed by Basu Bhattacharya went on to win the National Film Award for Best Feature Film and was also nominated for the Grand Prix at the Moscow Film Festival in 1967. Name the film?

21) This romantic thriller in the backdrop of terrorism was screened at the Helsinki Film Festival and went on the win the Netpac Award at the Berlin International Film Festival in 1999. Name this film?

22) This movie directed by Sonali Bose won a National Award for Best Feature Film in English. It also won Teenage Choice Award at Cine Donne Film Festival in Torino, Italy. Name this film?

23) This film is based on the life of Subir Banerjee, who played the role of Apu in Ray's classic 'Pather Panchali'. The film went on to win the Best Director Award for Kaushik Ganguly at the International Film Festival of India (IFFI). Name the film?

24) This Telegu film directed by K Vishwanath won the Prize of the Public at the Besancon Film Festival of France in 1981. The film also won National Film Awards in India. Name the film?

25) This iconic film made by Satyajit Ray went on to win a Golden Lion at Venice Film Festival in 1957. Name the film?

26) This film directed by Satyajit Ray, set in the background of rural Bengal during World War 2 went on to win the Golden Bear for Best Film at the Berlin International Film Festival in 1973. Name the film?

27) This was Shaji N Karun's debut film and went on to win the Golden Camera (Special Mention) at the 1989 Cannes Film Festival. Name the film?

28) Satyajit Ray won 2 Silver Bears at the Berlin International Film Festival in 1964 and 1965. Name the films for which he got the awards?

29) This film directed and produced by Adoor Gopalakrishnan went on to win the UNICEF Award at

the Venice Film Festival in 1990. It also won 4 National Awards in the same year. Name the film?

30) This film directed by Shaji N Karun won the Sir Charles Chaplin Award at the Edinburgh Film Festival in 1989. Name the film?

31) This film directed by Rituparno Ghosh won the NETPAC Award at the Berlin Film Festival in 2000. Kiron Kher won a National Film Award for Best Actress for her work in this film. Name the film?

32) He is one of the three filmmakers to win the Silver Bear for Best Director twice at Berlin Film Festival. He is also the second person after Charlie Chaplin to be awarded an honorary doctorate by the Oxford University. Name this iconic director?

33) This film based on the Bombay bombings of 1993 went on to win the Grand Jury Prize at the Indian Film Festival of Los Angeles. The Censor Board did not allow the film to be released in India for 2 years. Name the film?

34) This film directed by Ritesh Batra went on to win the Critics Week Viewers Choice Award at the Cannes Film Festival. The film features Irrfan as a lonely accountant about to retire. Name the film?

35) Who won the Best Supporting Actor Award for the film 'Angshumaner Chhobi' at the 54th Asia Pacific Film Festival?

36) She made her debut as a costume designer in the film CID (1956). She was later nominated for a BAFTA Award for Best Costume Design for the film Gandhi. Name this well known costume designer?

37) This talented music composer won his first Golden Globe Award for Slumdog Millionaire. He won his

second Golden Globe Award for the film '127 Hours'. Name this iconic music director?

38) This film highlights the life of Mumbai underworld and the plight of bar girls. Tabu won a Best Actress Award at the India International Film Festival for this film. Name the film?

39) This film is set in the background of feudal life in Kerala and is considered one of Adoor Gopalakrishnan's prominent films. This film also won the Sutherland Trophy at the London Film Festival in 1982. Name the film?

40) This film directed by Buddhadeb Dasgupta won a National Award for Best Bengali film in 1987 and was also nominated for a Golden Bear at the Berlin Film Festival in 1988. Name the film?

41) This Tamil film directed by Mani Ratnam went on to win the Best Film Award at the Belgrade Film Festival in 1997. The film starred Mohanlal, Prakash Raj and Aishwarya Rai. Name the film?

42) This film directed by Mani Ratnam set in the background of riots in Bombay in 1992 went on to win the Gala Award at the Edinburgh International Film Festival in 1995. Name the film?

43) Ritesh Batra won the Best Screenplay Award and Jury Grand Prize at the Asia Pacific Screen Awards for which film?

44) Who won the Best Actor – Feature at the Dubai International Film Festival for the movie 'The Lunchbox'?

45) This Hindi film directed by Partho Sen Gupta was never released in India due to censor board issues.

The film went on to win the Best Film Award at the Durban International Film Festival. Name the film?

46) This iconic Satyajit Ray classic has won the National Film Award for Best Feature Film and also the Sutherland Award for Best Original and Imaginative Film at the British Film Institute Awards in 1960. Name the film?

47) This film directed by Mrinal Sen won the National Film Award for Best Feature Film and also the Silver Prize at the 9th Moscow International Film Festival in 1975. Name the film?

48) This film directed by Mrinal Sen starring Shabana Azmi, Naseeruddin Shah and Pankaj Kapur won the Best Film Award at the Chicago International Film Festival. The film is based on a novel by Premendra Mitra. Name the film?

49) For which film was Raj Kapoor nominated for the Grand Prize at the Cannes Film Festival?

50) He has been awarded the Legion of Honour by the French Government and is the winner of the Lifetime Achievement Award during the 4th Asian Film Awards in Hong Kong. Name this iconic superstar of Indian cinema?

Chapter Six – Film Awards in India

6   Film Awards in India

With Indian cinema completing a century a look back at the work produced shows some remarkable films made in the different industries (Bollywood, Tollywood etc) over the years. There have been numerous categories of Awards to recognize contribution to cinema as well. These awards fall in 2 categories - Government awards like Dada Saheb Phalke Awards and National Film Awards and industry body awards like Filmfare, Screen Awards etc. There are also regional awards like Karnataka State Film Awards, Tamil Nadu State Film Awards and critic's awards like Bengal Film Journalists Association Awards.

National Film Awards remains one of the most prestigious awards for cinema in India. It was started in 1954 and is considered the Indian equivalent to the American Academy Awards. It is awarded at a ceremony in Delhi where the President of India gives away the awards. National Film Awards capture both feature and non-feature films. The feature film awards include Swarna Kamal for Best Feature Film, Best Director, Best Children's Film, Best First Film of a Director, Best Animated Film and Best Popular Film providing wholesome entertainment. Similarly Rajat Kamal is awarded for Best Actor, Best Actress, Best Audiography, Best Supporting Actor, Best Supporting Actress and other categories.

Tamil Nadu State Film Awards were started in 1967 and are given to recognize talents in the South Indian film industry. The award categories include – Best Film, Best Director, Best Family Film, Best Actor, Best Actress, Best Villain, Best Comedian, Best Child Artist etc. The awards have been discontinued since 2008.

Karnataka State Film Awards are awarded by Government of Karnataka to honour talent in the Kannada film industry. The categories include Best Film, Best Social Film, Best Children Film, Best Regional Film, Best Director, Best Actor, Best Actress, Best Supporting Actor, Best Supporting Actress, Best Music Director etc.

The Bengal Film Journalists Association is the oldest association of film critics in India and was founded way back in 1937. It awards includes numerous categories like Best Indian Films, Best Director, Best Actor, Best Actress, Best Supporting Actor, Best Supporting Actress, Best Screenplay, Best Cinematographer, Best Editor, Best Music Director etc.

Questions –

1) In which year was the National Film Award for the Best Film Critic instituted?

2) He was one of the founders of the Calcutta Film Society. He went on to win the National Film Award for Best Critic in 1986. Name him?

3) What is special about Anupama Chopra's book 'Sholay – the making of a classic'?

4) This film won the National Award for Best Hindi Film and also won the leading actress a Filmfare Award for Best Actress (Critics). It was also awarded the Best Indian Film Award by the Bengal Film Journalists Association and is based on the life of an ill-fated actress. Name this film?

5) Who won the Tamil Nadu State Film Award for Best Actor in 1996 and for which film?

6) This iconic film directed by Mani Ratnam also launched the career of a great music director who went on to win multiple awards like National Film Award for Best Music Direction, Filmfare Award for Best Music Director – Tamil and Tamil Nadu State

Film Award for Best Music Director. Name the music director and the film?

7) In which year was the National Film Award for the Best Investigative film instituted?

8) Bhupen Hazarika's claim to fame was as a singer. But he also went on to win the National Award for Best Feature Film in Assamese in 1961. Name the film?

9) Who won the National Film Award for Best Child Actor for Mira Nair's 'Salaam Bombay'?

10) For which film did Vanraj Bhatia win the National Film Award for Best Music Direction?

11) Who holds the record for highest number of Best Direction awards at the National Film Awards till 2014?

12) Name the first film to win National Film Award for Best Film?

13) This film based on a novel by Shankar and best in the setting of a electric fan industry, went on to win the National Film Award for Best Film in 1971. Name the film?

14) Name the first Tamil film to win the National Film Award for Best Film?

15) He directed a film based on the life of a steeplechase National Champion who later turned into a dacoit. This film helped the director win the National Film Award for Best Film. Name the director?

16) A graduate of the National School of Drama. Winner of National Film Award for Best Actor in 2012 and Filmfare Best Supporting Actor in 2007. Name this talented actor?

17) He has directed movies like 'Electric Moon' which won the National Film Award for Best Film in English. He has also written a field guide on trees in Delhi. Name this multi-faceted director turned environmentalist?

18) This film set in the backdrop of School of Planning and Architecture went on to win the National Film Award for Best Film in English. Name this iconic film?

19) Who won the National Film Award for Best Film in 1997 for the film 'Lal Darja' and was a professor of economics before taking up a career in film making?

20) This film directed by Adoor Gopalakrishnan deals with a young man's belief in communism and went on to win the National Film Award for Best Film in 1996. Name this film?

21) K Balachander won the National Film Award for Best Feature Film in Tamil in 1969 for a film starring Gemini Ganesan. Name the film?

22) In which year was the Tamil Nadu State Film Award for Best Film started?

23) Who won the National Film Award for Best Supporting Actor for Ray's classic 'Ghare Baire' in 1984?

24) Who won the National Film Award for Best Chid Artist for the film 'Mera Naam Joker'?

25) Satyajit Ray has won many National Awards for Best Feature Film and Best Director. Ray won the National Award for Best Music Direction in 1973. Name the film for which he won the Award?

26) Who won the National Film Award for Best Female Playback Singer for the film 'Hum Hain Rahi Pyar Ke' in 1993?

27) He won a Filmfare Award for Best Movie for the film 'Kabhi Haan Kabhi Naa'. He also won the National Film Award for Best First Film of a Director. Name this talented director?

28) This award winning director won two back to back National Awards for Best Director in 1979 and 1980. Name this director?

29) He started his career with a TV cookery show, Khana Khazana. He went on to win the National Film Award for Best Direction in 2013. Name this director?

30) In which year was the National Film for Best Film on Environment Conservation instituted?

31) He came to Mumbai from Aurangabad. He initially worked in theatre before moving to films. He has directed films like Tukaram and Bindhaast. He went on the win the National Film Award for Best Film in Marathi. Name this director?

32) This film directed by Sonali Bose featured Konkona Sen Sharma and politician Brinda Karat. It went on to win the National Film Award for Best Feature Film in English. Name this film?

33) Who directed the film 'Looking Back' which won the National Film Award for Best Industrial Film in 1987?

34) In which year was the National Film Award for Best Story instituted?

35) Who won the National Film Award for Best Story in 1974 for the movie 'Jukti Takko Aar Gappo'?

36) He is well known Indian film critic and documentary film maker. He writes in English and Malayalam. He has been awarded the National Film Award for Best Film Critic in 2009. Name this critic?

37) This animated film directed by Nikhil Advani went on to win the National Film Award for Best Animated Film in 2012. Name this film?

38) Who was the first recipient of National Film Award for Best Actress in 1967?

39) This talented actress was born in Andhra Pradesh but made her mark in Malayalam films. She went on to win 3 National Film Awards for Best Actress. Name this talented actress?

40) This talented actress has won a record 5 National Film Awards for Best Actress. She won this prestigious award three times in a row between 1982 and 1984. Name this actress?

41) This talented actor was the first recipient of the National Film Award for Best Actor in 1967. Name this brilliant actor?

42) Who won the National Film Award for Best Actor in 2010 for the Tamil film 'Aadukalam'?

43) What is common to Kamal Haasan, Mammootty and Amitabh Bachchan?

44) This film directed by Tapan Sinha went on to win the National Film Award for Best Children's Film in 1977. Name this film?

45) Till date which director has won the most number of National Awards for Best Direction?

46) Aparna Sen has won the National Award for Best Direction twice. Name the 2 films for which she has been awarded?

47) Who won the National Film Award for Best First Film of a Director for the film 'Chittagong'?

48) Who won the National Film Award for Best Supporting Actor for the film 'Raakh' in 1988?

49) Who won the National Film Award for Best Supporting Actor for the film 'Rock On' in 2008?

50) He is a well known Tamil actor. He won the National Film Award for Best Supporting Actor for the film 'Azhagarsamiyin Kudhirai'. Name this actor?

51) He was a well known cinematographer and went on to work in 21 of Satyajit Ray's films. He also won 3 National Awards for Best Cinematography in the 1970's. Name this cinematographer?

52) Who is the first recipient of the National Award for Best Supporting Actress for the film Party?

53) Only two actresses till date have won the National Film Award for Best Actress and Best Supporting Actress. Name them?

54) This film set in the background of emergency shows the oppression of jute mill workers in Kolkata. The film went on to win the National Film Award for Best Film in 1982 and also Best Director Award. Name the film?

55) This film directed by Rituparno Ghosh went on to win the National Award for Best Feature Film. It is based on the Ingmar Bergman film 'Autumn Sonata'. Name the film?

56) This film directed by Shyam Benegal is set in a Madhya Pradesh village. It based on a novel by Harsh Mander. The film went on to win the National Film Award for Best Feature Film in 1998. Name the film?

57) Who won the National Award for Best Female Playback Singer for the movie 'Antaheen'?

58) Name the well known actor and singer who won the NTR National Award in 2002?

59) This film directed by Cheran won the National Award for Best Popular Film Providing Wholesome Entertainment and Filmfare Award South for Best Tamil Film in 2004. Name the film?

60) This film directed by Rosshan Andrrews is set in a boarding school in Ooty and revolves around the life of 3 students. It went on to win the Filmfare South Award for Best Film in Malayalam. Name the film?

61) This film directed by Ajoy Kar went on to win the National Film Award for Best Feature Film in Bengali in 1957. It is based on the Hollywood film 'Random Harvest'. Name the film?

62) Who won the Special Jury Award for Non Feature film at the National Film Awards in 1980 for 'The Chola Heritage'?

63) This film directed by Ashvin Kumar tells the story of contemporary Kashmir. The film went on to win the National Film Award for Best Investigative Film in 2012. Name the film?

64) This film by herpetologist Romulus Whitaker and Shekhar Dattari on snake catchers went on to win the National Film Award for Best Scientific Film in 1987. Name the film?

65) This award was instituted at the 32nd National Film Awards in 1984 and lastly awarded in 1988. Name the category of Film Awards?

66) Anupama Chopra is a well known author and film critic. What award did she win for her book 'Sholay: The Making of a Classic'?

67) This documentary film directed by Satyajit Ray on Benod Behari Mukherjee a blind artist and teacher at Visva Bharati University went on to win the National Film Award for Best Non Feature Film in 1972. Name the film?

68) Filmmaker Gaurav Jani's solo motorcycle trip from Mumbai to Ladakh became a journey of self discovery and went on to become a documentary film on Chang pas of Ladakh. Name this film that went on to win the National Film Award for Best Non Feature Film in 2005?

69) Who won the National Film Award for Best Supporting Actor for the film 'Mirch Masala' in 1986 directed by Ketan Mehta?

70) This talented singer has won 7 National Awards for Best Male Playback Singer in 3 languages – Malayalam, Telegu and Hindi. Name this singer?

Chapter Seven – Indian Movies at the Oscars

7   Indian Movies at the Oscars

Indian films have been associated with the Oscars for a long time. 5 Indians have won 6 Oscars till date. Indian Films have been participating since 1958 in the Best Foreign Film category. While there have been controversies surrounding the selection of films that went on to represent India at the Oscars, there can be no doubt that some great films have been nominated and some have missed out as well. In recent year movies like Lunch Box and Kahani were tipped to make it but failed to make the cut. The closest an Indian film has got to winning an Oscar in the Foreign Language category was when 'Mother India' lost out by just 1 vote.

Questions –

1) Which iconic Hindi film was India's first nomination for the Oscars in the Best Foreign Language film?

2) Who was the first Indian to win an Oscar?

3) Along with Bhanu Athaiya another Indian was nominated for an Oscar from the same film Gandhi (1982). Name this genius?

4) Name the only Indian to win 2 Oscars till date?

5) Name the first Indian and only Indian till date to win an Honorary Oscar for Lifetime Achievement?

6) This iconic actor has been part of 7 films that have been sent as India's nominations to the Oscar. He is yet to win one. Name this actor?

7) This epic film set in the times of British Raj became nominated for the Best Foreign Language film. It

failed to win the award but the film was a huge hit. Name this film?

8) What is common to the movies 'Apur Sansar', 'Mahanagar' and "Shatranj Ke Khiladi' apart from the fact that all these movies were directed by Satyajit Ray?

9) This film based on the lives of street children of Bombay went on to be nominated for an Oscar for Best Foreign Language film and was voted by New York Times as among the Best 1000 Movies ever made. Name the film?

10) Name the only Indian director to win an Oscar and to have 3 of his films to represent the country as the official entry for the Oscars?

11) In 2011 AR Rahman won another Oscar nomination for Best Original Score for this film. Name this film featuring the adventures of canyoning hiker?

12) Time Magazine rated this film in the list of Bollywood classics. The film was based on a novel by R.K.Narayan and went on to become India's official entry into the Oscars. Name this film?

13) Time Magazine included this film in its list of 'All Time 100 Best Films'. This film directed by Mani Ratnam won the National Film Award for Best Film and was also India's official entry for the Oscars. Name the film?

14) Name 3 films featuring Aamir Khan that have been India's official entry to the Oscars?

15) This film directed by Anusha Rizvi based on farmer suicides went on to become India's official entry for the Oscars. Name this satirical film?

16) Barfi was India's official entry for the Oscars in 2012. What was the original name for this film directed by Anurag Basu?

17) She was born in Kolkata and grew up in Mumbai. A well known Carnatic music vocalist and music composer, she was nominated for Best Original Song for the movie 'Life of Pi' at the Oscars. Name the singer/composer?

18) He was born in Gujarat and went on to direct, act and produce Hindi Films. He won National Awards as well as was nominated for the Best Foreign Language Film at the Oscars in 1958. Name the director?

19) Mother India was the first Indian nomination at the Oscars and came the closest to win in the category of Best Foreign Language Film. Which film did it lose to by a single vote?

20) What is common to Akira Kurosawa, Satyajit Ray, Sophia Loren, Peter O'Toole and Greta Garbo?

21) This Indo-Canadian film maker was nominated for the Academy Award for Best Foreign Language film. She was born in India and studied at Lady Shri Ram College for Women. Name this talented director?

22) He was born in Mumbai and later moved to the US. He went on to be nominated for Best Feature Film at the Academy Awards for the film 'The Remains of the Day'. Name this iconic director and producer?

23) Till date of all the Indian films showcased at the Oscars, only 3 films have been nominated for Best Foreign Language Feature Film. Name these films?

24) This Malayalam film directed by CG Rajendra Babu was India's official entry to the Oscars in 1997. Name this film starring Mohanlal?

25) This Hindi film directed by Bimal Roy was India's entry to the Oscars in 1958. The screenplay was by Ritwik Ghatak and Rajinder Singh Bedi and starred Dilip Kumar and Vyjayantimala. Name this film?

26) This film directed by Chetan Anand was India's official entry to the Oscars in 1967. This was also Rajesh Khanna's debut film. Name the film?

27) The only film directed by Hrishikesh Mukherjee to be nominated as India's entry to the Oscars was?

28) Manthan is a film set in the background of India's White Revolution (Operation Flood). It was also India's official entry to the Oscar in 1977. The film was directed by Shyam Benegal. Who wrote the story for the film apart from Shyam Benegal?

29) The film 'Shatranj Ke Khiladi' directed by Satyajit Ray was India's official entry to the Oscars in 1978. The film is based on a book of the same name written by?

30) This film directed by Mahesh Bhatt was India's entry to the Oscars in 1985. This was also the debut film of Anupam Kher. Name the film?

31) This sound designer is a graduate of FTII, Pune. He got his first break with Black, a Hindi film. Later he went on to win an Oscar for Best Sound Mixing for the film 'Slumdog Millionaire'?

32) In 2001 Lagaan was nominated for the Best Foreign Language Feature Film at the Oscars. Name the movie that won the Award?

33) This film won the Nation Film Award for Best Telegu film in 1986. It was directed by K Vishwanath and is the only Telegu film to be India's official entry for the

Oscars in the Best Foreign Language film category. Name the film?

34) Who played the role of Shashi Godbole in the film 'English Vinglish' which was India's official entry to the Oscar Awards in 2012?

35) This film starring Sivaji Ganesan in a triple role was India's official entry to the Oscars in 1969. Jayalalitha played the female lead. Name the film?

36) This Tamil film directed by S Shankar was India's entry to the Oscars in 1998 and starred Prashanth and Aishwarya Rai. Name the film?

37) This film directed by Sanjay Leela Bhansali was the most expensive Hindi film of its time. It was India's official entry to the Oscars and was also nominated for the BAFTA Award for Best Foreign Language film in 2003. Name the film?

38) This Malayalam film featuring Salim Kumar and Zarina Wahab was India's official entry to the Oscars in 2011. It was the debut film of Salim Ahamed. Name the film?

39) Name the only Indian director to have 3 of his films selected as India's official entry to the Oscars for the Best Foreign Language film?

40) Name the apex body that shortlists and selects the Indian film to be nominated as official entry to the Oscars in the Best Foreign Language film category?

41) This film directed by Mani Ratnam won 3 National Awards and was based on the story of a dying mentally disabled child. The film was nominated as India's official entry to the Oscars in the Best Foreign Language Film category. Name the film?

42) This film directed by Deepa Mehta is based on Bapsi Sidhwa's novel 'Cracking India' and went on to become India's official entry to the Oscars. Name the film?

43) This film directed by Kamal Haasan was based on India's partition and Gandhi's assassination. The film was nominated as India's official entry to the Oscars. Name the film?

44) This film directed by Geetu Mohandas and starring Nawazuddin Siddiqui and Geetanjali Thapa was India's official entry to the Oscars in 2014. Name the film?

45) This film directed by Ashvin Kumar was nominated for Live Action Short Film in 2005. The film is based on a story of a Pakistani boy who crosses the border while fetching a cricket ball. Name the film?

46) This film directed by Shekhar Kapur was based on the life of the bandit Phoolan Devi and went on to become India's official entry to the Oscars in 1994. Name the film?

47) This film directed by Bharathan went on to win 5 National Awards and was also India's official entry to the Oscars in 1992. It was later remade in Hindi as Virasat. Name the film?

48) This film directed by Sandeep Sawant was the first Marathi film to be nominated as India's official entry to the Oscars. The film also won the National Film Award for Best Film in 2004. Name the film?

49) This film directed by Subhendu Roy is based on Tagore's short story 'Samapti'. The film was India's official entry to the Oscars in 1972. Name the film?

50) Name the two films of director Subhendu Roy which were nominated as India's official entry to the Oscars in 1972 and 1973?

Chapter Eight - Indian English Films

8   Indian English Films

While Hindi and Regional films have flourished in India over the last century, there has been a limited market for English films made in India. While Hollywood movies find a market in urban India, Indian made English films are few and far between. Some Hollywood and British movies have been shot in India like Gandhi, Octopussy, A Passage to India, Namesake etc. There have been some significant Indian English films as well like 36 Chowringhee Lane, 15 Park Avenue, English August, Hyderabad Blues etc. Then there is a genre of English films with Indian subjects shot in England or America like Bend it Like Beckham, East is East, Namesake etc. In the last 30 years there has been a steady flow of Indian films made in English by notable directors like Aparna Sen, Dev Benegal, Pradip Krishen and others.

Questions –

1) Who directed English August?

2) Who acted as Justice Chatterjee in Joggers Park?

3) Who wrote the screenplay for 36 Chowringhee Lane?

4) Which film won the Best Feature Film in English at the National Film Wards in 1995?

5) Which Indian actor is referred to as 'Sean Penn of Oriental cinema'?

6) Who played the role of Varun in Hyderabad Blues 2?

7) Who composed the music for the film 36 Chowringhee Lane?

8) Which film won the Nargis Dutt Award for Best Feature Film on National Integration?

9) The movie 'Bow Barracks Forever' is based on which community?

10) Which rock band is featured in the movie 'Bong Connection'?

11) Who played the role of coach 'Joe' in the movie 'Bend it like Beckham?

12) Which film won the Best comedy film at the British Comedy Awards in 2002?

13) This movie directed by Rituparno Ghosh won the National Award for Best Feature Film in English?

14) Which 1980's film is set in the backdrop of School of Planning and Architecture in Delhi?

15) Who acted as well as wrote the screenplay for the movie 'In Which Annie Gives it Those Ones'?

16) What was Saif Ali Khan's first movie in English?

17) Rituparno Ghosh acted in this award winning English film? Name the film?

18) Amol Palekar won the National award for directing this bilingual film in English and Marathi?

19) Who played the role of Violet Stoneham in the film '36 Chowringhee Lane'?

20) This actress played the role of young Violet in '36 Chowringhee Lane'. She later quit films to focus on theatre. Who is she?

21) She was born in Pune. She is well known for her contribution to theatre. She has acted in films like

Monsoon Wedding and The Best Exotic Marigold Hotel. Name the actress?

22) Bow Barracks Forever, a film by Anjan Dutt is set in which Indian city?

23) This film deals with an award winning photographer in the process of undergoing a cornea transplant and its aftermath. It also went on to win the National Film Award for Best Film. Name this film?

24) He won the National Film Award for Best Picture with his 3rd film. His first film was 'Right Here, Right Now'. Name this talented director?

25) This film directed by Mahesh Dattani explored Carnatic music, raga and contemporary Indian music. Name the film?

26) This actress was educated in New York City. She made her film debut in Nagesh Kukunoor's 'Bollywood Calling'. Name this actress?

27) Who played the role of Johnny Mathew, the PT instructor in the film 'Rockford'?

28) This film directed by Revathi went on to win the National Film Awards for Best Film and featured Shobana and Nasir Abdullah. Name the film?

29) Who played the role of Meethi in Aparna Sen directed '15 Park Avenue'?

30) Daughter of a RBI employee, this actress played the role of Gulbadan in the Hindi film 'Rangeela'. She later went on to win the Best Supporting Actress for Rituparno Ghosh's 'Last Lear'. Name the actress?

31) This film directed by Shyam Benegal went on the win the National Film Award for Best Feature Film in

English. It was based on the book 'Apprenticeship of a Mahatma' by Fatima Meer. Name this movie?

32) Dr.Barasaheb Ambedkar won the National Film Award for Best Feature Film in English. Who directed this movie?

33) Who played the role of Dr.Kunal Barua in the film '15 Park Avenue' directed by Aparna Sen?

34) Which English Film directed by Unni Vijayan is based on the novel 'Lessons in Forgetting' by Anita Nair?

35) Who played the role of J.A.Krishnamoorthy in the film 'Lessons in Forgetting'?

36) This film directed by Prakash Belawadi featured Anant Nag and Suhasini. It went on to win the National Film Award for Best Feature Film in English. Name the film?

37) Who played the role of Malti Srivastava in the film 'English August' directed by Dev Benegal?

38) Who played the role of Boltu in the movie 'Electric Moon' directed by Pradeep Krishen?

39) She wrote the screenplay for the movie 'In Which Annie Gives It Those Ones' and also played the role of Radha in the same film. Name this writer and actor?

40) The movie 'In Which Annie Gives It Those Ones' won 2 National Awards – one for Best Feature Film in English. What was the second category for which it was awarded?

41) Who played the role of Lalita Bakshi in Gurinder Chadda's 'Bride and Prejudice'?

42) This film directed by Avantika Hari was based on the issue of honour killings. The film went on to win the

National Film Award for Best Feature Film in English. Name the film?

43) Who played the role of Kamla Devi in Pamela Rook's 'Miss Beatty's Children'?

44) Who played the role of Sita Avery in Dev Benegal's 'English August'?

45) Who played the role of Raja Chowdhury, a wildlife photographer in Aparna Sen directed 'Mr and Mrs Iyer'?

46) He worked on first English serial on Indian television called 'Mouthful of Sky'. He also directed films like 'Mumbai Matinee' and 'Joggers Park'. Name the talented director?

47) Who played the role of Anjali in Aparna Sen directed '15 Park Avenue'?

48) She is a well known author and activist and she wrote the screenplay for the film 'Electric Moon' directed by Pradip Krishen. Name this activist and author?

49) Who played the role of Ranveer in Pradip Krishen directed film 'Electric Moon'?

50) Who won the National Film Award for Best Actor for Shyam Benegal's 'Making of Mahatma'?

Chapter Nine – General Movie Quiz

9   General Movie Quiz

This chapter covers a general movie quiz with 30 questions each with multiple choices as answers. So time to get your brain cells to work again. Happy quizzing!

Questions –

1) Which Indian actor has played the role of Captain Nemo in the Hollywood film 'The League of Extraordinary Gentlemen'?

a) Om Puri

b) Naseeruddin Shah

c) Paresh Rawal

d) Victor Banerjee

2) Who played the role of Dominic Pinto in the Hindi film 'Albert Pinto Ko Gussa Kyoon Aata Hain'?

a) Naseeruddin Shah

b) Satish Shah

c) David Dhawan

d) Pankaj Kapur

3) Who won the Filmfare Award for Best Comedian for the film 'Jaane Bhi Do Yaaro'?

a) Ravi Baswani

b) Naseeruddin Shah

c) Satish Shah

d) Rajesh Puri

4) Who won the National Award for Best Supporting Actor for the film 'Mirch Masala'?

a) Raj Babbar

b) Om Puri

c) Mohan Gokhale

d) Suresh Oberoi

5) Which film directed by Ketan Mehta was nominated for the Golden Prize at the Moscow International Film Festival?

a) Hero Hiralal

b) Mirch Masala

c) Aar Ya Paar

4) Holi

6) The well known music director Pritam Chakraborty completed his graduation from which college?

a) Ferguson College, Pune

b) Hindu College, Delhi

c) Presidency College, Kolkata

d) St.Xaviers, Kolkata

7) The Tamil star Shivaji Rao Gaekwad is better known as?

a) Sivaji Ganesan

b) Madhavan

c) Prabhu Deva

d) Rajnikanth

8) Soumitra Chatterjee has acted in how many films directed by Satyajit Ray?

a) 7

b) 10

c) 12

d) 14

9) Uttam Kumar made his debut in a Bengali film that was never released. Name the film?

a) Dristhidan

b) Mayador

c) Nayak

d) Basu Paribar

10) Who played the role of Dharmadihkari in the Kannada film 'Accident' directed by Shankar Nag?

a) Shankar Nag

b) Anant Nag

c) Ramesh Bhat

d) Srinivas Prabhu

11) Who played the role of young Vijay Deenanath Chauhan in Agneepath?

a) Amitabh Bachchan

b) Master Manjunath

c) Alok Nath

d) Avtar Gill

12) Who won the National Film Award for Best Female Playback Singer for the Telegu film 'Swati Kiranam'?

a) Kavita Krishnamurthy

b) Vani Jayaram

c) Asha Bhonsle

d) K.S.Chithra

13) Who played the role of Berkeley in the National Award winning Assamese film 'Chameli Memsaab'?

a) Victor Banerjee

b) Anil Chatterjee

c) George Baker

d) Tarun Kumar

14) Bhupen Hazarika the National Award Music director studied Political Science at which college?

a) BHU

b) Hindu College

c) Cotton College

d) City College

15) This Hindi's films soundtrack became the first Bollywood soundtrack to reach top 10 album sales for the iTunes Store. Name the film?

a) Dil Chahta Hain

b) Don

c) Rab Ne Bana Di Jodi

d) Rock On

16) Who played the role of Chitragupta in the comedy film 'Quick Gun Murugan'?

a) Rajendra Prasad

b) Vinay Pathak

c) Ranvir Shorey

d) Raju Sundaram

17) He has won the Jayadeb Puraskar in 1999 and Orissa State Film Award for Best Actor for Phula Chandana. Name the talented Oriya actor?

a) Prashanta Nanda

b) Sriram Panda

c) Uttam Mohanty

d) Bijay Mohanty

18) Who played the role of Quick Gun Murugan in the comedy film 'Quick Gun Murugan'?

a) Rajendra Prasad

b) Vinay Pathak

c) Ranvir Shorey

d) Raju Sundaram

19) He won the National Film Award for Best Film in Telegu for Bharya Bhartalu (1962). Later he won the Dada Saheb Phalke Award. Name this talented producer/director?

a) Ramana Reddy

b) L.V.Prasad

c) B.N.Reddy

d) B. Nagi Reddy

20) This talented lyricist wrote over 8000 songs spanning over 350 Hindi films. He was later awarded the Dada Saheb Phalke Award. Name this lyricist?

a) Majrooh Sultanpuri

b) Kavi Pradeep

c) Naushad

d) Vasant Dev

21) Which eminent Bollywood director has written the book 'A Taste of Life – The Last Days of U.G.Krishnamurti'?

a) Vishal Bharadwaj

b) Govind Nihalini

c) Mahesh Bhatt

d) Amol Palekar

22) What was Anupam Kher's debut film?

a) Saaransh

b) Utsav

c) Arjun

d) Karma

23) Who directed the film 'Everybody Says I'm Fine'?

a) Aparna Sen

b) Rahul Bose

c) Dev Benegal

d) Kaizad Gustad

24) Who played the role of Tarak, a foley artist in Kaushik Ganguly directed 'Shabdo'?

a) Srijit Mukherjee

b) Kaushik Sen

c) Ritwik Chakraborty

d) Victor Banerjee

25) Who wrote the book 'First Day, First Show' on the Bollywood film industry?

a) Anupama Chopra

b) Rajesh Devraj

c) Sangita Gopal

d) Jerry Pinto

26) Which was the first Tamil film to win the National Film Award for Best Feature Film?

a) Nayagan

b) Marupakkam

c) Roja

d) Kanchivaram

27) Who was the National Film Award for Best Actor for the film Rickshawkaran?

a) M.G.Ramachandran

b) Kamal Hasaan

c) Sivaji Ganesan

d) Cho Ramaswamy

28) What was the real name of fictional detective Feluda created by Satyajit Ray?

a) Ajit Banerjee

b) Prodosh Sen

c) Prodosh Chandra Mitra

d) Lalmohan Ganguly

29) Popularly known as the 'Showman', he won 2 National Film Awards and his performance in Awaara was ranked by Time magazine as one of the 10 greatest performances. Name the actor?

a) Dilip Kumar

b) Raj Kapoor

c) Dev Anand

d) Kishore Kumar

30) Name 2 siblings who have won the Dada Saheb Phalke Award?

a) Ashok Kumar and Kishore Kumar

b) Lata Mangeshkar and Asha Bhonsle

c) B.R.Chopra and Aditya Chopra

d) Dev Anand and Chetan Anand

10   The Answers

Chapter 2 – Section 2.1 (The Early Years) Answers

1) Alam Ara

2) Alam Ara produced by Ardeshir Irani was released.

3) Fearless Nadia acted in all these films.

4) Himansu Rai started Bombay Talkies in 1934.

5) Sulochana

6) Dhoop Chhaon

7) Kisan Kanya (1937)

8) Chittor Nagaiah

9) Sant Tukaram was screened at the 1937 Venice Film festival.

10) Prithviraj Kapoor

11) Ashok Kumar and Devika Rani

12) Devika Rani

13) Zinda Lash

14) Kundan Lal Saigal

15) Pramathesh Barua

16) Jamuna Barua

17) Pankaj Mullick

18) Pankaj Mullick

19) Irada (1944)

20) Jagte Raho (1956)

21) Raj Kapoor

22) Dilip Kumar

23) Ruma Guha Thakurta

24) Kishore Kumar

25) Devika Rani

26) Karma (1933)

27) Saraswati Devi

28) Sikandar (1941)

29) Sulochana

30) Sohrab Modi

31) Naushad

32) Lata Mangeskar

33) Majrooh Sultanpuri

34) Chitralekha (1941)

35) Swaran Lata

36) Debaki Bose

37) Chandra Mohan

38) Anil Biswas

39) Ashok Kumar

40) Nargis

Chapter 2 – Section 2.2 (Movies after 1947) Answers

1) Suchitra Sen

2) Prahaar where there is a Colonel VK Singh.

3) Parveen Babi.

4) Chupke Chupke is a remake of "Chadmabesi" released in 1971.

5) S.D Burman

6) RD Burman

7) Kishore Kumar

8) Vijeta

9) Both had institutional backers. Manthan (National Diary Development Board) and Susman (Handloom Co-operatives)

10) Ashish Vidyarthi

11) Sandip Patil

12) Haqeeqat (1964)

13) Harindranath Chattopadhyay

14) Hrishikesh Mukherjee

15) Utpal Dutt

16) Rajesh Khanna

17) Kishore Kumar

18) Sharmila Tagore

19) Keshto Mukherjee

20) David Abraham Cheulkar

21) Amitabh Bachchan

22) Jaya Bachchan

23) All these actors studied at the FTII, Pune

24) Gautam Joglekar

25) Farooq Shaikh

26) Hrishikesh Mukherjee

27) Mithun Chakraborty

28) K A Abbas

29) Sangam (1964) and Mera Naam Joker (1970)

30) Raj Kappor

31) Lalkaar (1972)

32) Dharmendra

33) These films featured the hit pair of Dharmendra and Hema Malini

34) Charas (1976)

35) Vijay Anand

36) Mahendra Kapoor and Lata Mangeshkar

37) Laxmikant and Pyarelal

38) Nutan

39) Anil Kapoor

40) Rakjumar Santoshi

41) Baat Ban Jaaye

42) Sanjeev Kumar

43) Dastak

44) Kamal Bose

45) Shahrukh Khan

46) Santosh Sivan

47) Preity Zinta

48) Qayamat Se Qayamat Tak

49) Sukhwinder Singh

50) Udit Narayan

51) Bharat Bhushan

52) Devdas, Madhumati and Bandini

53) Kanoon (1960)

54) Yaadein (1964)

55) Sunil Dutt

56) Ashok Kumar

57) Hamraaz (1967)

58) Helen

59) Manna Dey

60) Om Puri

Chapter 2 – Section 2.3 (The New Millennium) Answers

1) Kaho Naa Pyaar Hai

2) Lucky Ali

3) Ajay Jadeja

4) Pran

5) Mir Ranjan Negi

6) Arjun Rampal

7) Chak De! India

8) Jaideep Sahni

9) Palash Sen of Euphoria

10) Aaja Nachle

11) Konkona Sen Sharma

12) An Affair to Remember

13) Naina Lal Kidwai's daughter Kemaya acted in Monsoon Wedding.

14) Jodha Akbar

15) Ashutosh Gowariker

16) Victory, a cricket based movie

17) New York

18) Pritam

19) Shaan

20) Indian Military Academy (IMA)

21) Mann

22) Anurag Basu

23) Pritam Chakraborty

24) Rajkumar Hirani

25) Ali Fazal

26) IIM Bangalore

27) Ghajini

28) Vinay Pathak

29) Kay Kay Menon

30) Rahul Bose

31) Raincoat (2004)

32) Dibakar Banerjee

33) Rock On

34) Koel Purie

35) 1971

36) Dil Chahta Hain directed by Farhan Akthar

37) Sonali Kulkarni

38) Kiran Rao

39) Rajat Kapoor

40) Suchitra Pillai

41) Jolly LLB

42) I Am

43) Sushant Singh

44) Amrish Puri

45) Black

46) He was won the National Award for both Black (Best Feature Film in Hindi) and Devdas (Best Popular Film for Providing Wholesome Entertainment)

47) Rani Mukherjee.

48) Neetu Singh

49) Konkona Sen Sharma

50) Mahi Gill

51) Nimrat Kaur

52) Irrfan Khan

53) Nawazuddin Siddiqui

54) Rani Mukerji

55) Aamir Khan

56) Taare Zameen Par

57) Akshaye Khanna

58) Amole Gupte

59) Divya Dutta

60) Kaminey

61) Santanu Moitra

62) Kunal Ganjawala

63) Ranveer Singh

64) Imtiaz Ali

65) Saif Ali Khan

66) Ranbir Kapoor

67) Deepika Padukone

68) Karan Johar

69) Kuch Kuch Hota Hain and My Name is Khan

70) Aditya Roy Kapur

71) Konkona Sen Sharma

72) Vidya Balan

73) Nishant Malkani

74) City Lights

75) Rajkummar Rao

76) Manoj Bajpai

77) Barry John

78) Metro Manila

79) Jimmy Shergill

80) Divya Dutta

81) Ajay Devgn

82) Raincoat (2004)

83) Khosla Ka Ghosla

84) Boman Irani

85) Ranvir Shorey

86) 1971

87) Manoj Bajpai

88) Farhan Akthar

89) Purab Kohli

90) Progeria – a genetic disorder which leads to quick acceleration of ageing process in children.

91) Arshad Warsi

92) Jhankaar Beats

93) I Am

94) Dil Chahta Hai

95) Udit Narayan

96) Raghu Romeo

97) Kai Po Che

98) Partho Gupte

99) All these films were produced by Ritesh Sidhwani

100) Sanjay Leela Bhansali

Chapter 3 – Bengali Movie Quiz Answers

1) Billamangal released on 8 November 1919.

2) Pather Panchali the first film directed by Satyajit Ray.

3) Suchitra Sen and Uttam Kumar

4) Mrinal Sen

5) Moloy Roy son of Monotosh Roy

6) Soumitra Chatterjee

7) Jhinder Bhandi

8) Arundhati Devi

9) Tulsi Chakraborty

10) Seemabaddha

11) Mayador

12) Martin Scorcese's 'Taxi Driver'

13) Waheeda Rehman

14) Sudhin Dasgupta

15) Soumitra Chatterjee

16) Chhabi Biswas

17) Satindra Bhattacharya

18) Kamu Mukherjee

19) Sonar Kella

20) Golpo Holeo Satyee

21) Abir Chatterjee

22) Paran Bandyopadhyay

23) Aranyer Din Ratri

24) Ritwik Ghatak

25) Madhabi Mukherjee

26) Badshahi Angti

27) Anjana Bhowmick

28) Supriya Devi

29) Shabdo

30) Rudranil Ghosh

31) Srijit Mukherjee

32) Barun Chanda

33) Suchitra Sen

34) Charulata

35) Harano Sur

36) Nimtita Raajbari, near Murshidabad

37) Ajoy Kar

38) Akash Kusum

39) Kushal Chakraborty

40) Tapan Sinha

41) Parapsychologist

42) Shabdo

43) Rituparna Sengupta

44) Srijit Mukherjee

45) Rituparna Sengupta

46) Kamaleshwar Mukherjee

47) Meghe Dhaka Tara

48) Podokkhep

49) Suman Ghosh

50) Aniruddha Roychowdhury

51) Parambrata Chatterjee

52) Indradeep Dasgupta

53) Abir Chaterjee

54) Payel Sarkar

55) Rupam Islam

56) Shreya Ghoshal

57) Hawa Bodol

58) Subhendu Chatterjee

59) Anjana Bhowmick

60) Samit Bhanja

61) Shunyo Awnko

62) Priyanka Bose

63) Priyanshu Chatterjee

64) Swastika Mukherjee

65) Kaushik Sen

66) Reshmi Ghosh

67) Sabyasachi Chakrabarty

68) Sabitri Chatterjee

69) Deepankar Dey

70) Kaushik Ganguly

71) Bhooter Bhabishyat

72) Paran Bandopadhyay

73) George Baker

74) Sreelekha Mitra

75) Saswata Chatterjee

76) Sourav Das

77) Rajatava Dutta

78) Neel Dutt

79) Mainak Bhaumik

80) Buno Haansh

81) Autograph

82) Nandana Sen

83) Rituparno Ghosh

84) Moner Manush

85) Priyanshu Chatterjee

86) Prosenjit Chatterjee

87) Royal Bengal Rahasya

88) Iti Mrinalini

89) Ushasie Chakraborty

90) Silajit Majumder

91) Anupam Roy

92) Rupankar Bagchi

93) Indrani Haldar

94) Ranjit Mullick

95) Shayan Munshi

96) Sagina Mahato

97) Anup Ghosal

98) Pratidwandi

99) Tapen Chatterjee and Rabi Ghosh

100) Bhalo Theko

101) Raja of Dharbhanga

102) Raja of Jaisalmer

103) Santosh Dutta

104) Siddhartha Chatterjee

105) Kamu Mukherjee

106) Mrinal Sen won Best Director at the National Film Awards for all these films

107) Akash Kusum

108)Anjan Dutt

109)Madly Bengalee

110)Apanjan

Chapter 4 – Regional Movies Quiz Answers

1) R Nataraja Mudaliar

2) Kalidas released in October 1931

3) Marmayogi

4) Mani Ratnam's 'Nayagan'

5) Chandralekha (1948)

6) Shivaji Ganesan

7) K Balachander

8) Adoor Gopalakrishnan

9) Sarika Thakur

10) Sita Bibaha (1936)

11) Sri Lokenath

12) Matira Manisha

13) Prasanta Nanda

14) Indradhanura Chhai

15) Nandita Das

16) No Award given in 2008

17) My Dear Kuttichathan (1984)

18) The Guard (2001)

19) Guru (1997)

20) Adoor Gopalakrishnan

21) Australia (1992)

22) Mohanlal

23) Mammooty

24) Juhi Chawla

25) Piravi

26) Doctor Bezbaruah

27) Chameli Memsaab

28) Assamese film industry

29) Joymoti

30) Jahnu Barua

31) Aparoopa (1982)

32) Agnisnaan

33) Biju Phukan

34) Moloya Goswami

35) Firingoti

36) Gonga Silonir Pakhi

37) Mon Jaai

38) Basundhara

39) Kannada film industry

40) Rajkumar

41) Shankar Nag

42) Bandhana

43) Laali

44) Bangarada Hoovu

45) Minchina Ota

46) Banker Margayya

47) Lokesh

48) Jeevana Chaitra

49) Shivarajkumar

50) Devaraj

51) Girish Kasaravalli

52) Monalisa

53) Bhalji Pendharkar

54) Baburao Painter

55) Shyamchi Aai

56) Sant Tukaram

57) Dada Konde

58) Shwaas

59) Bhaskar Chandavarkar

60) Ashwin Chitale

61) Raghupati Venkaiah Naidu

62) Patala Bhairavi

63) Bhisma Pratigna

64) Bhakta Prahlada

65) Gharana Mogudu

66) Gabbar Singh (2012)

67) Swati Mutyam

68) Sankarabharanam

69) S P Balasubrahmanyam

70) Narsinh Mehta

71) Naseeruddin Shah

72) Bhavni Bhavai

73) Gunasundari

74) Akhand Saubhagyavati

75) Pooja na Phool

76) Kanchivaram

77) Balayogini

78) Baby Saroja

79) Muthu

80) Paruthiveeran

81) Jyothika

82) Kamal Haasan

83) Mani Ratnam

84) Kathantara

85) Dwaar

86) Zerifa Wahid

87) Uttam Mohanty

88) Chilika Teerey

89) Gharabaher

90) Dombivali Fast

Chapter 5 – Indian Films at Film Festivals Quiz Answers

1) Rohini Hattangadi

2) 'Song of the Road (Pather Panchali) directed by Satyajit Ray in 1958

3) Aparajito and Apur Sansar

4) Amar Bhoopali

5) Do Bigha Zamin

6) Kharij

7) Anjan Dutt

8) Chorus

9) Basu Bhattacharya

10) Silver Bear – Special Jury Prize

11) Amar Bhuban

12) Hatey Bazarey

13) Raghuvir Yadav

14) Phera

15) Uttara

16) Adoor Gopalakrishnan

17) Satyajit Ray

18) Mrigayaa

19) Svayamvaram

20) Teesri Kasam

21) Dil Se

22) Amu

23) Apur Panchali

24) Sankarabharanam

25) Aparajito

26) Asani Sanket

27) Piravi

28) Mahanagar and Charulata

29) Mathilukal

30) Piravi

31) Bariwali

32) Satyajit Ray

33) Black Friday

34) Lunch Box

35) Soumitra Chatterjee

36) Bhanu Athaiya

37) A R Rahman

38) Chandni Bar

39) Elippathayam

40) Phera

41) Iruvar

42) Bombay

43) The Lunchbox

44) Irrfan Khan

45) Hava Aney Dey

46) Apur Sansar

47) Chorus

48) Khandhar

49) Awara

50) Amitabh Bachchan

Chapter 6 – Film Awards in India Quiz Answers

1) 1984

2) Chidananda Dasgupta

3) This book won the National Film Award for the Best Book on Cinema

4) Zubeida directed by Shyam Benegal

5) Kamal Haasan for Indian

6) AR Rahman for Roja

7) 1990

8) Shakuntala

9) Shafiq Syed

10) Tamas (1987)

11) Satyajit Ray has won this award 6 times

12) Shyamchi Aai (Marathi) was the first film to win the award in 1953

13) Seemabaddha directed by Satyajit Ray

14) Marupakkam (1990)

15) Timangshu Dhulia for Paan Singh Tomar

16) Irrfan Khan

17) Pradip Krishen

18) In Which Annie Gives it Those Ones

19) Buddhadeb Dasgupta

20) Kathapurushan

21) Iru Kodugal

22) 1967

23) Victor Banerjee

24) Rishi Kapoor

25) Ashani Sanket

26) Alka Yagnik

27) Kundan Shah

28) Mrinal Sen

29) Hansal Mehta

30) 1989

31) Chandrakant Kulkarni

32) Amu

33) Prakash Jha

34) 1964

35) Ritwik Ghatak

36) C.S.Venkiteswaran

37) Delhi Safari

38) Nargis for Raat Aur Din

39) Sharada

40) Shabana Azmi

41) Uttam Kumar

42) Dhanush

43) All these actors have won the National Film Award for Best Actor 3 times

44) Safed Haathi

45) Satyajit Ray has won this award 6 times

46) 36 Chowringhee Lane and Mr. and Mrs.Iyer

47) Bedabrata Pain

48) Pankaj Kapur

49) Arjun Rampal

50) Appukutty

51) Soumendu Roy

52) Rohini Hattangadi

53) Konkona Sen Sharma and Sharmila Tagore

54) Chokh

55) Unishe April

56) Samar

57) Shreya Ghoshal

58) Dr.Rajkumar

59) Autograph

60) Notebook

61) Harano Sur

62) Adoor Gopalakrishnan

63) Insha'Allah Kashmir

64) A Cooperative for Snake Catchers

65) National Film Award for Best Industrial Film

66) National Film Award for Best Book for Cinema

67) The Inner Eye

68) Riding Solo to the Top of the World

69) Suresh Oberoi

70) K.J.Yesudas

Chapter 7 – Indian Films at the Oscars Quiz Answers

1) Mother India in 1958 was India's first entry

2) Bhanu Athaiya in 1983 for Best Costume Design

3) Pandit Ravi Shankar

4) A R Rahman for Best Original Score and Best Original Song

5) Satyajit Ray

6) Kamal Haasan

7) Lagaan

8) All these films were India's official entry to the Oscars in their respective years

9) Salaam Bombay

10) Satyajit Ray

11) 127 Hours

12) Guide

13) Nayakan

14) Lagaan, Rang De Basanti and Taare Zameen Par

15) Peepli Live

16) Khamoshi

17) Jayashri Ramnath

18) Mehboob Khan

19) Nights of Cabiria (Italian film)

20) They are all recipients of the Academy Honorary Award

21) Deepa Mehta

22) Ismail Merchant

23) Mother India, Salaam Bombay and Lagaan

24) Guru

25) Madhumati

26) Aakhri Khat

27) Majli Didi (1968)

28) Dr.Verghese Kurien (father of Operation Flood)

29) Munshi Premchand

30) Saaransh

31) Resul Pookutty

32) Lagaan lost to Bosnian film 'No Man's Land'

33) Swati Mutyam

34) Sridevi

35) Deiva Magan

36) Jeans

37) Devdas

38) Adaminte Makan Abu

39) Satyajit Ray

40) Film Federation of India

41) Anjali

42) Earth

43) Hey Ram

44) Liars Dice

45) Little Terrorist

46) Bandit Queen

47) Thevar Magan

48) Shwaas

49) Uphaar

50) Uphaar and Saudagar

Chapter 8 – Indian English Movie Quiz Answers

1) Dev Benegal.

2) Victor Banerjee

3) Aparna Sen

4) English August

5) Rahul Bose

6) Nagesh Kukunoor

7) Vanraj Bhatia

8) Mr and Mrs.Iyer

9) Anglo Indian community

10) Cassini's Division

11) Jonathan Meyers

12) Bend it Like Beckham

13) The Last Lear

14) In Which Annie Gives It Those Ones

15) Arundhati Roy

16) Being Cyrus

17) Memories in March

18) Quest

19) Jennifer Kendal

20) Sanjana Kapoor

21) Lilette Dubey

22) Kolkata

23) Ship of Theseus

24) Anand Gandhi

25) Morning Raga

26) Perizaad Zorabian

27) Nagesh Kukunoor

28) Mitr, My Friend

29) Konkona Sen Sharma

30) Shefali Shah

31) The Making of the Mahatma

32) Jabbar Patel

33) Dhritiman Chatterjee

34) 'Lessons in Forgetting'

35) Adil Hussain

36) Stumble

37) Tanvi Azmi

38) Raghubir Yadav

39) Arundhati Roy

40) Best Screenplay Award

41) Aishwarya Rai

42) Land Gold Women

43) Protima Bedi

44) Mita Vashisht

45) Rahul Bose

46) Anant Balani

47) Shabana Azmi

48) Arundhati Roy

49) Roshan Seth

50) Rajit Kapoor

Chapter 9 – General Movie Quiz Answers

1) Naseeruddin Shah

2) David Dhawan

3) Ravi Baswani

4) Suresh Oberoi

5) Mirch Masala

6) Presidency

7) Rajnikanth

8) 14

9) Mayador

10) Anant Nag

11) Master Manjunath

12) Vani Jayaram

13) George Baker

14) BHU

15) Rab Ne Bana Di Jodi

16) Vinay Pathak

17) Uttam Mohanty

18) Rajendra Prasad

19) L.V.Prasad

20) Majrooh Sultanpuri

21) Mahesh Bhatt

22) Saraansh

23) Rahul Bose

24) Ritwik Chakraborty

25) Anupama Chopra

26) Marupakkam

27) M.G. Ramachandran

28) Prodosh Chandra Mitra

29) Raj Kapoor

30) Lata Mangeshkar and Asha Bhonsle

Appendix A – List of Dada Saheb Phalke Winners

Dada Saheb Phalke Award is the country's highest award in cinema. The award is named in honour of Dadasaheb Phalke maker of India's first full length feature film Raja Harishchandra. The Awards are present at the National Film Awards ceremony. Devika Rani was the first recipient of this prestigious award and Gulzar is the most recent awardee. Prithviraj Kapoor is the only posthumous recipient of this award. The table below gives the complete list of Awardees till date –

Year Awarded	Recipient	Film Industry
1969	Devika Rani	Hindi
1970	Birendranath Sircar	Bengali
1971	Prithviraj Kapoor	Hindi
1972	Pankaj Mullick	Bengali, Hindi
1973	Ruby Myers (Sulochana)	Hindi
1974	Bommireddy Narasimha Reddy	Telegu
1975	Dhirendra Nath Ganguly	Bengali
1976	Kanan Devi	Bengali
1977	Nitin Bose	Bengali, Hindi
1978	Raichand Boral	Bengali, Hindi
1979	Sohrab Modi	Hindi
1980	Paidi Jairaj	Hindi, Telegu
1981	Naushad	Hindi
1982	L.V.Prasad	Hindi, Tamil, Telegu
1983	Durga Khote	Hindi, Marathi
1984	Satyajit Ray	Bengali
1985	V Shantaram	Hindi, Marathi

1986	B.Nagi Reddy	Telegu
1987	Raj Kapoor	Hindi
1988	Ashok Kumar	Hindi
1989	Lata Mangeshkar	Hindi, Marathi
1990	Akkineni Nageswara Rao	Telegu
1991	Bhalji Pendharkar	Marathi
1992	Bhupen Hazarika	Assamese
1993	Majrooh Sultanpuri	Hindi
1994	Dilip Kumar	Hindi
1995	Rajkumar	Kannada
1996	Shivaji Ganesan	Tamil
1997	Kavi Pradeep	Hindi
1998	B.R.Chopra	Hindi
1999	Hrishikesh Mukherjee	Hindi
2000	Asha Bhosle	Hindi, Marathi
2001	Yash Chopra	Hindi
2002	Dev Anand	Hindi
2003	Mrinal Sen	Bengali
2004	Adoor Gopalakrishnan	Malayalam
2005	Shyam Benegal	Hindi
2006	Tapan Sinha	Bengali, Hindi
2007	Manna Dey	Bengali, Hindi
2008	V.K.Murthy	Hindi
2009	D Ramanaidu	Telegu
2010	K Balachander	Tamil, Telegu
2011	Soumitra Chatterjee	Bengali
2012	Pran	Hindi
2013	Gulzar	Hindi

Appendix B – Leading Directors of Indian Cinema

Satyajit Ray -

Satyajit Ray was born in Calcutta in May 1921. He graduated from Presidency College, Kolkata and then went to Visva-Bharati University at Santiniketan. He worked as a junior visualiser in a British firm. He started the Calcutta Film Society in 1947 along with Chidananda Dasgupta. He went on to direct more than 30 films and documentaries. He is the most awarded Indian director in the history of Indian cinema. His first film 'Pather Panchali' won the Best Human Document at the Cannes Film Festival. His classic works include Apu Trilogy, Calcutta Trilogy, Nayak, Ghare Baire, Aranyer Din Ratri and Abhijan. He was an awarded an honorary in 1992 for his contributions to world cinema. He has also been awarded Bharat Ratna and Dada Saheb Phalke Award. He has won 32 National Film Awards in different categories. He used to also run the Sandesh magazine for children started by his grandfather Upendrakishore Ray. He has penned numerous stories like the Feluda series, Professor Shonku etc. He passed away in 1992. Ray's son Sandip is also a well know film maker in Bengal.

Mrinal Sen –

Mrinal Sen was born in Calcutta in May 1923. He studied Physics at Scottish Church College and later got his Masters at Calcutta University. He worked briefly as a medical representative before working as an audio technician in Calcutta film studio. Sen has directed 27 films in a period spanning almost 50 years. Mrinal Sen has won 8 National Film Awards and numerous awards at International Film Festivals like the Silver Prize at Moscow International Film Festival for Chorus and Parashuram, Berlin International Festival for Akaler Sandhane, Jury Prize at Cannes Film Festival for Kharij and numerous other awards. In 2005 he was awarded the Dada Saheb Phalke Award. He is also recipient of Padma Bhushan. He was awarded the Order of Friendship by President Vladimir Putin. He completed his autobiography 'Always Being Born' in 2004. Along with Ray and Ghatak his contemporaries, Sen is considered one of the finest exponents of Indian parallel cinema.

Ritwik Ghatak –

Ritwik Ghatak was born in Dhaka in East Bengal (now Bangladesh) in November 1925. His family moved to Calcutta before the partition in 1947. Ghatak joined the Indian People's Theatre Association (IPTA) in 1951. He made his first film Nagarik in 1952. He tasted commercial success as a script writer with Hindi film 'Madhumati' (1958) directed by Bimal Roy. Ghatak briefly taught at the Film and Television Institute in Pune in the 1960's. Ghatak's well known films include Ajantrik, Subarnarekha, Meghe Dhaka Tara, Komal Gandhar and Jukti Takko Aar Gappo. He won a National Film Award for Jukti Takko Aar Gappo. He was awarded Padma Shri for Arts by Government of India. He also won the Best Directors Award from Bangladesh Cine Journalist's Association for Titash Ekti Nadir Naam. He passed way in 1976.

Tapan Sinha -

Tapan Sinha was born in Calcutta in the month of October 1924. He studied Physics at the University of Patna and did his Masters at the University of Calcutta. He started his career as a sound engineer and later went to England in 1950 where he worked in the Pinewood Studios for 2 years before returning home. He went on to direct over 30 films primarily in Bengali and a few films in Hindi and Oriya. His films have won a plethora of National Awards and International Awards at film festivals. He has won National Film Awards for his films Kabuliwala, Hatey Bazarey, Atithi, Ek Doctor Ki Maut, Louha Kapat and Kshudhita Pashan. He was also awarded the Dada Saheb Phalke Award in 2006. Some of his International Awards include Best Film for Kshudhita Pashan at Cork

Festival – Ireland, International Certificate of Merit at the Venice Film Festival for Atithi, Afro-Asian Award at Moscow Film Festival for Sagina Mahato.

He passed away in 2009.

Buddhadeb Dasgupta –

Buddhadeb Dasgupta was born in 1944 at Anara near Purulia in West Bengal. He studied economics at the Scottish Church College and at University of Calcutta. He briefly taught economics before moving to film direction. His debut film was 'Dooratwa'. He has directed more than 15 feature films and over 10 documentaries. He has won numerous National Film Awards for his films like Bagh Bahadur, Charachar, Lal Darja, Kaalpurush, Phera, Uttara, Sapner Din, and Tahader Katha. He won Best Direction for 2 films – Uttar and Sapner Din. He has won numerous nominations at International Film Festivals like Golden Bear nomination for Phera and Charachar at the Berlin International Film Festival. Uttar was nominated for the Golden Lion at the Venice Film Festival. He is an accomplished poet with numerous books published on poetry like Sreshtha Kabita, Govir Araley etc. He was honoured with Lifetime Achievement Award at the Spain International Film Festival in Madrid in 2008.

Adoor Gopalakrishnan –

Adoor Gopalakrishnan was born in July 1941 at the village of Pallickal near Adoor, Kerala. He has played a pivotal role in transforming Malayalam cinema and is considered as one of best directors in India. After securing a degree in Economics and Political Science he briefly worked in the Government before joining FTII, Pune in 1962. He won a National Award with his debut film Swayamvaram (1972). He was won numerous National Film Awards for Best Film, Best Director, Best Screenplay, Best Book on Cinema, and Special Jury Award for Non Feature Film. He was won the Best Director for 5 films namely – Swayamvaram, Mukhamukham, Anantharam, Mathilukal and Nallu Pennungal.

He has won numerous Kerala State Film Awards for Best Film, Best Director, Best Story, Best Screenplay, Best Documentary Film and Best Book on Cinema. He has been awarded the Dada Saheb Phalke Award in 2004. He was awarded the Legion of Honour by the French Government. He has won numerous awards at International Film Festivals like Sutherland Trophy for Elippathayam at the London Film Festival. He also won the British Film Institute Award for the same film. He has been awarded the Lifetime Achievement Award at the Cairo International Film Festival.

Shyam Benegal –

Shyam Benegal was born in Secunderabad in December 1934. He did his master in economics from Nizam College, Osmania University. He founded the Hyderabad Film Society. He had a brief stint in the advertising industry before teaching at the FTII, Pune between 1966 and 1973. He started making documentaries like 'Child of the Streets' which won him wide acclaim. Benegal's debut film Ankur won him a National Film Award for Second Best Feature Film and was also selected as India's official entry to the Oscars. Some of his other notable films to win National Awards include Nishant, Manthan, Junoon, Arohan, Trikaal, Suraj Ka Satva Ghoda, Mammo, Samar, Zubeida and The Forgotten Hero. He also won the National Film Award for Best Feature Film in English for 'The Making of Mahatma' and National Film Award for Best Feature Film in Urdu for Sardari Begum. He has shot over 30 documentary films including the award winning biographical film on Satyajit Ray. He has been recognized internationally as well. Nishant was nominated for the Golden Palm at the Cannes Film Festival. Kalyug won the Golden Prize at the Moscow International Film Festival in 1981.

He was awarded the Dada Saheb Phalke Award in 2005.

V Shantaram –

V Shantaram was born in Kolhapur, Maharashtra in November 1901. He started his career doing odd jobs in Maharashtra Film Company. He later acted in silent films and became an actor. He acted in films like Sinhagad, Dr.Kotnis Ki Amar Kahani, Amrit Manthan and Stri. He later became a director and producer. His well known films include Aadmi, Jhanak Jhanak Payal Baaje, Navrang, Stri, Do Aankhen Barah Haath, Maali etc. He won National Awards for Jhanak Jhanak Payal Baaje, Do Aankhen Barah Haath. He also won a Filmfare Award for Best Director for the movie Jhanak Jhanak Payal Baaje. His films were also recognized in international film festivals like Sliver Bear at the Berlin International Film Festival for Do Aankhen Barah Haath. He also received a nomination for Grand Prize at the Cannes Film Festival for the film 'Amar Bhoopali'. He was awarded the Dada Saheb Phalke Award for lifetime contribution to Indian cinema in 1985. He passed away in October 1990. He was posthumously awarded the Padma Vibhusan in 1992.

Hrishikesh Mukherjee –

Hrishikesh Mukherjee was born in Kolkata in September 1922. He completed his graduation in Chemistry from University of Calcutta and later taught mathematics for some time. He worked as a cameraman and editor at New Theatre in Calcutta before moving to Mumbai to work under his mentor Bimal Roy. His debut film was Musafir (1957). He later went on to direct many memorable films like Anuradha, Anupama, Aashirwad, Anand, Guddi, Bawarchi, Namak Haram, Milli, Chupke Chupke, Golmaal and Khoobsoorat. He won National Awards for his films Musafir, Anari and Anuradha. He also won Filmfare Awards for Anand, Khoobsoorat, Anokhi Raat and Madhumati. He was a well known editor and won a Filmfare Award for Best Editing for Madhumati. His movies had connected with middle class issues and are seen even today. He also won a Golden Bear nomination for Anuradha at the Berlin International Film

Festival. He won the Dada Saheb Phalke Award in 1999 for his contribution to Hindi cinema. He passed away in 2006.

Mani Ratnam –

Mani Ratnam was born in Madurai, Tamil Nadu in June 1956. Mani grew up in Chennai and graduated in Commerce from Ramakrishna Mission Vivekananda College. He later did his MBA from Jamnalal Bajaj Institute of Management studies in Mumbai. He worked as a management consultant for a few years before joining films. He comes from a family of film producers. His debut film was a Kannada movie Pallavi Anu Pallavi in 1983. This film won a Karnataka State Film Award for Best Screenplay. He later went on to direct memorable films like Nayagan. Geethanjali, Thalapathi, Roja, Bombay, Dil Se, Kannathil Muthamittal, Saathiya, Yuva, Guru. He gave a break to debutant music director AR Rahman in Roja. He won numerous National Film Awards for films like Mouna Ragam, Geethanjali, Anjali, Roja, Bombay, and Kannathil Muthamittal. He also won numerous Filmfare Awards for Guru, Saathiya, Bombay, Thalapathi, and Mouna Ragam. Nayagan was included in Time magazines 'All Time 100 Greatest Movies' in 2005. He has won numerous international awards like Gala Award at Edinburgh Film Festival for Bombay, NETPAC Award for Dil Se at Berlin International Film Festival, Best Picture Award at Zimbabwe International Film Festival for Kannathil Muthamittal. He won the Padma Shri in 2002.

Bimal Roy -

Bimal Roy was born in July 1909 in Suapur, East Bengal (now part of Bangladesh). He moved to Calcutta and worked as a camera assistant at New Theatre. He assisted Promotesh Barua with the making of classic Devdas. He later moved to Bombay. He went on to make memorable films in Hindi like Do Bigha Zamin, Parineeta, Biraj Bahu, Madhumati, Sujata and Bandini. He won numerous National Film Awards for film like Do Bigha Zamin, Biraj Bahu, Devdas, Madhumati, Sujata and Bandini. He also won the international recognition by winning the International Prize at the Cannes Film

Festival for Do Bigha Zamin. He also won nomination for the Grand Prize at Cannes for Do Bigha Zamin. He won 9 Filmfare Awards for Madhumati a record that stood for almost 4 decades. He died of cancer in 1965.

References and Further Reading –

- http://www.lemauricien.com/article/hundred-years-indian-cinema-silent-movies-talkies

- http://realityviews.blogspot.in/2012/10/list-of-280-bollywood-hindi-movies.html

- http://www.adoorgopalakrishnan.com/profile.htm

- http://upperstall.com/films/1993/indradhanura-chhai

- http://www.imdb.com/name/nm0159350/bio

- http://www.telegraphindia.com/1090121/jsp/entertainment/story_10417517.jsp

- http://en.wikipedia.org/wiki/BAFTA_Award_for_Best_Film

- Indian Film Festival of Melbourne http://www.iffm.com.au/

- BAFTA Award for Best Film - http://en.wikipedia.org/wiki/BAFTA_Award_for_Best_Film

- Academy Honorary Awardees - http://en.wikipedia.org/wiki/Academy_Honorary_Award

- National Film Award for Best Feature Film - http://en.wikipedia.org/wiki/National_Film_Award_for_Best_Feature_Film

- Mahanayak Revisited – The World of Uttam Kumar by Swapan Kumar, Tranquebar 2013.

- Our Films, Their Films – Satyajit Ray, Orient Black Swan

- Encyclopedia of Hindi Cinema, by Govind Nihalani, Saibal Chatterjee, Gulzar. Popular Prakashan, 2003.

- Indian Cinema : The World's Biggest and Most Diverse Film Industry - http://www.cornerhouse.org/wp-content/uploads/old_site/media/Learn/Study%20Guides/Indian%20cinema.pdf

- Sun Mere Bandhu Re – The Musical World of S.D.Burman by Sathya Saran, Harper Collins India 2014

- Great Masters of Indian Cinema: The Dadasaheb Phalke Award Winners, by D. P. Mishra, Publications Division, Ministry of Information and Broadcasting, Govt. of India, 2006.

- Conversations with Mani Ratnam by Rangan Baradwaj, Penguin Books India 2012

- Childhood Days – A Memoir by Satyajit Ray, translated from Bengali by Bijoya Ray, Penguin 1998

- Gulzar; Nihalani, Govind; Chatterjee, Saibal (2003). Encyclopedia of Hindi Cinema. Encyclopedia Britannica (India) Pvt Ltd.

- Rinki Roy Bhattacharya (2009). Bimal Roy: The Man who spoke in pictures. Penguin Books Limited.

- Shyam Benegal (BFI World Directors) – Sangeeta Dutta, British Film Institute 2003

- Films of Buddhadeb Dasgupta by John W.Hood Orient Blackswan 2005

- Encyclopaedia Britannica article on Mrinal Sen - http://www.britannica.com/EBchecked/topic/762851/Mrinal-Sen

- Tamil Cinema - http://www.culturopedia.com/cinema/tamil_cinema.html

- History through the lens – Perspectives on South Indian Cinema by S Theodore Baskaran, Orient Blackswan 2009

- Adoor Gopalakrishnan : A Life in Cinema by Gautaman Bhaskaran, Penguin Books India 2010

- Profiles, five film makers from India: V Shantaram, Raj Kapoor, Mrinal Sen, Guru Dutt, Ritwik Ghatak by Shampa Banerjee, Directorate of Film Festivals, NFDC 1985.

Index

A - Assamese p8,42,48,52,53,58,71,97 Acchot Kanya p11, Apradhi p12, Alexander p13, Apna Ghar p14, Amrit Manthan p14,138, Aradhana p15, Air Force Academy p15, Aakhri Khat p16, Amarkant Varma p19, Ashok Kumar p11,20,62,102, Anand p20, Ardh Satya p21, Allan Border p22, Ashish Nehra p22, An Affair to Remember p22, Ankur Arora Murder Case p23, Anupam Kher p24,82,100,, Agent Vinod p24, Aamir Khan p26,80, Ali Abbas Zaffar p27, Ayan Mukerji p28, Action Replay p28, Aisha Banerjee p28, A Wednesday p29, Amrit Sagar p30, Aditya Shroff p30, Auro p31, Abhishek Kapoor p31, Arjun Harishchand Waghmare p31, Aparna Sen p 8,34,39,44,46,75,87,89,90,91,100,, Aniruddha Roy Choudhury p8,34,43,, Anik Dutta p34,42, Anjan Dutta p34,44,46,, Abhijan p35,134, Anthony Hope p35, Akash Kusum p36,40,,22, Annapurnar Mandir p36,, Abir Chatterjee p37, Ashutosh College p40, Arekta Din p40, Aranyer Din Ratri p41,134, Aborto p41, Aguntuk p42, Anando p42, Assam p42,53, Aschorjo Prodip p42,43,, Aamra p43,, Autograph p43,44, Abhiroop Sen p43, Arekti Premer Golpo p43, Abar Byomkesh p44, Andy p45, Akaler Sandhane p46,62,134, Anjan Sen p46, Ayodhyecha Raja p49, Afro Asian Film Festival p50, Ajeyo p52, Agnisnan p52, Accident p53,96, Anant Nag p54,90,96, Asha Parekh p57, Arun Bhatt p57, Ameer Sultan p57, Abhimaan p58, Adoor Gopalakrishnan p8,61,63,64,66,72,136,, Asia Pacific Film Festival p62,65, Apu p64, Angshumaner Chhobi p65, Aishwarya Rai p66,83, Asia Pacific Screen Awards p66, Asian Film Awards p67, American Academy Awards p69, Anupama Chopra p70,77,101, Aurangabad p73, Andhra Pradesh p74, Aadukalam p74, Amitabh Bachchan p74,96, Azhagarsamiyin Kudhirai p75, Autumn Sonata p75, Antaheen p76, Ajoy Kar p76, Ashvin Kumar p76,84, Apur Sansar p80, A.R. Rahman p80,139, Anusha Rizvi p80, Anurag Basu p81, Akira Kurusawa p81, A Passage to India p87, America p87, Amol Palekar p88,99, Apprenticeship of a Mahatma p90, Anita Nair p90, Avantika Hari p90, Anjali p91, Albert Pinto Ko Gussa Kyoon Aata Hain p93, Aar Ya Paar p94, Alok Nath p96, Avtar Gill p96, Asha Bhonsle p96,102, Anil Chatterjee p97, A Taste of Life - The Last Days of U.G.Krishnamurti p99, Arjun p100, Ajit Banerjee p101, Awaara p102, Aditya Chopra p102.

B - Bombay Talkies (film) p7, Bombay Talkies (production house) p11, Bhakt Prahlad p9, Bharat Ratna p14,134, Bharat Bhusan p14,23, Badshah Humayun p14, Bollywood

p72, Ghare Baire p72,134, Gaurav Jani p77, Gujarat p18,81, Greta Garbo p81, Geetu Mohandas p84, Geetanjali Thapa p84, Gulbadan p89, Gurinder Chadda p90, George Baker p97,

H - Hindustan Hamara p12, Hemant Kumar p12, Humayun p14, Hum Hindustani p18, Hrishikesh Mukherjee p19,20,82,138, Howrah Bridge p20, Harbhajan Singh p22, Helen Keller p25, Hawa Hawai p27,31, Hindi4,7,8,10,11,12,13,14,15,17,18,19,20,21,22,23,24,25,27, 28,30,31,35,36,41,42,45,50,52,66,70,77,79,81,82,83,84,87,89 ,93,97,99,135,139, Hindu College p27,95,97, Hum Tum p27, Hum Panch p28, Hansal Mehta p28,29, Hiralal Sen p34, Hollywood p18,38,59,76,87,93, Hawa Bodol p40, Hari p41, Hemanter Pakhi p41, Haat Baraley Bandhu p42, Hemlock Society p44, Hirak Rajar Deshe p45, Harishchandrachi Factory p49, The Harikrishnan's p51, Hiren Bora p53, H.M.Reddy p56, Hey Ram p58, Hyatulla Ansari p61, Helsinki Film Festival p64, Hong Kong p67, Hum Hain Rahi Pyar Ke p73, Herpetologist p76, Honorary Oscar p79, Hyderabad Blues p87, Hyderabad Blues 2 p87, Hero Hiralal p94, Holi p94,

I – Izzat p11, Inquilab p12, Indian Grand Prix p21, 3 Idiots p23, Imperial College of Engineering p23, ISI p24, Indira p26, IIFA Award p28,29, Indian Institute of Management, Calcutta p28, Ishq Mein Jeena Ishq Mein Marna p29, International Film Festival of India p39,64, ICFAI Business School p40, Interview p44, Indian Panorama p53, Indrajit Lankesh p55, India International Film Festival p56,66, Indian Film Festival of Los Angeles p61, Indian Film Festival of Melbourne p61, International Prize p62,139, Irrfan p65, Ingmar Bergman p75, Indo-Canadian p81, In Which Annie Gives it Those Ones p88,90, iTunes p97,

J - Jwar Bhatta p12, Jhansi Ki Rani p13, Jugnu p18, Johnny Mera Naam p18, Joy Lobo p23, Jamshedpur p27,41, Jab We Met p27, Jagdish Tyagi p31, Jolly LLB p31, Juhi Chawla p31, Jaane Kyon p31, Jamai Shasthi p34, Joy Baba Felunath p35,45, Jekhane Bhuter Bhoy p36, Jukti Takko Aar Gappo p37,73,135, Jalsaghar p38, Jaya Bhaduri p41, Jhilik Bose p41, Jyotirindranath Tagore p41,43, Jaatishwar p41,44, Jawl Phoring p44, Jadavpur University p44, Jara Bristite Bhijechhilo p44, Jaisalmer p45, Jyoti Prasad Agarwala p48, Joymati p48, Japanese p17,50,57, Jollywood p52, Jahnu Barua p48,52,53, Jury Prize p62, Jury Grand Prize p66, Jayalalitha p83, Justice Chatterjee p87, Joggers Park p87,91, Joe p88, Johnny Mathew p89, J.A.Krishnamoorthy p90, Jaane Bhi Do Yaaro p93, Jayadeb Puraskar p98, Jerry Pinto p101,

K - Kannada 4,8,27,48,53,54,69,96,139, K.L.Saigal p12, Karlovy Vary International Film Festival p12, Karma p13,100, Khoon Ka Khoon p13, Kabhi Ajnabee The p15, Kisi Se Na Kehna p16, Koshish p19, Kai Po Che p21, Khosla Ka Ghosla p21,30, Kolkata p24,41,45,46,75,81,138, Kuch Kuch Hota Hain p25,28, Kusum Duggal p25, Karan Johar p28, Kishen Khurana p30, Khamoshi p32, Kaushik Ganguly p34,37,64,100, Kabuliwala p38,135, Kamaleshwar Mukherjee p39, Kolkata Medical College p40, Konkona Sen Sharma p41,44,73, Karam Apnaa Apnaa p41, Kailashey Kelenkari p41, King of Shundi p45, King of Halla p45, Kharij p46,134, Keechaka Vadam p48, Kerala p48,66,136, Ketan Mehta p49,57,77,94, Kamal Haasan p50,56,74,84,101, Kalapani p51, Karnataka State Film Awards p54,55,69,139, Kalpana p54, K Raghavendra Rao p56, K Vishwanath p56,64,82, Kushi p58, Kapil Bora p58, Kiron Kher p65, K Balachander p72, Kabhi Haan Kabhi Naa p73, Khana Khazana p73, Kashmir p76, Kahani p79, Kamla Devi p91, Kavita Krishnamurthy p96, K.S.Chithra p97, Kavi Pradeep p99, Kaizad Gustad p100, Kaushik Sen p100, Kanchivaram p101, Kishore Kumar p102,

L - Life of Christ p9, Lalkaar p17, Lakshya p22,30,32, Lagaan p24,82, Legend of Bhagat Singh p25,29, Love Aaj Kal p27, London Dreams p28, Love Sex and Dhoka p29, Luck By Chance p32, Lady Brabourne College p39, Lalan Fakir p43, Legion of Honour p63,67,137, London Film Festival p66,137, Lal Darja p72,136, Looking Back p73, Ladakh p77, Life of Pi p81, Lady Shriram College for Women p81, Live Action Short Film p84, Last Lear p89, Lessons in Forgetting p90, Lalita Bakshi p90, L.V.Prasad p99, Lyricist p14,37,99, Lalmohan Ganguly p102, Lata Mangeshkar p102,

M - Malayalam p4,8,48,50,51,74,76,77,81,83,136, Marathi p4,8,27,48,49,55,56,59,61,73,84,88, Miss Frontier Mail p11, Manzil p12, Mukti p12, Mehboob Khan p14, Mere Sapno Ki Rani p15, Manthan p15,82,105,137, Mrinal Sen p8,16,34,36,38,40,44,46,50,61,62,63,67,134, Mithun Chakraborty p17, Mera Naam Joker p17,72, Mala Sinha p17, Major Ram Kapoor p17, Meri Jung p18, Mission Impossible 18, Mumbai p18,20,23,24,29,56,66,73,77,81,91,138, Mirza Ghalib p19, Mother India p20,79,81, Major Chandrakant p20, Mumtaz p20, Mera Naam Chin Chin Chu p20, Madhuri Dixit p21, Mr and Mrs Iyer p21,91, Mann p22, Monsoon Wedding p22,24,89, Martin Crowe p22, Mere Yar Ki Shaadi p22,29, Main Aisa Kyu Hun p22, Memento p23, Murder p27, Miley Jab Hum Tum p28, Magistrate Wilkinson p29, Maachis p29, Munna Bhai p29, My Name is Khan p29, 3 Mistakes of My Life p31, Mainak Bhaumik p34,43, Meghe Dhaka Tara p37,40,135, Madly Bangalee p37, Mishawr Rahashyo p39, Maoist p41, Moner Manush p41,43, Miss India Earth p41, Mr. Ramsey p42, Maach Misti and More p43, Madrid International Film Festival p44, Macchli Baba p45, Mere Apne p46, Malaysia p48, Mohan Sundar Deb Goswami p49, M.G.Ramachandran p49,101, Marlon Brando of Indian Cinema p50, Manmadha Leelai p50, Mohanlal p51,66,81, Mammooty p51,74, Maine Gandhi Ko Nahi Mara p52, Malgudi Days p53, Maharashtra

Film Company p55,138, Moscow Film Festival p56,61,62,63,94,136,137, Maharaja Dhiraj Chandrasen p57, Madurai p57,139, Michael Douglas p59, Mira Nair p61,71, Mani Ratnam p,66,70,83,139, Madhya Pradesh p14,76, Mirch Masala p77,94, Mahanagar p80, Mahesh Bhatt p82,99, Mahesh Dattani p89, Meethi p89, Malti Srivastava p90, Miss Beatty's Children p91, Mouthful of Sky p91, Mumbai Matinee p91, Making of the Mahatma p91,137, Mohan Gokhale p94, Madhavan p95, Mayador p95, Master Manjunath p96, Majrooh Sultanpuri p99, Marupakkam p101,

N - National Film Awards p8,16,21,34,38,49,55,58,62,69,71,74,77,89,102,134,135,136, 139, Nartaki p14, Nanda p20, New Zealand p21, Naina Lal Kidwai p22, New York p22, Naseem p23, National School of Drama p26,63,71, Nawab p27, Naina Talwar p28, Nar Singh p35, Nayak p36,43,46,96,134, Nita p37, Nostonir p38, Nirbhoya p42, New York Indian Film Festival p44, Nandita Das p49, Narsinh Mehta p49, Nua Bou p50, N.T.Rama Rao p56, Nirupa Roy p57, Nayagan p58,101,139, Nishikant Kamat p59, Neecha Nagar p61,62, NETPAC Award p64,65,139, Naseeruddin Shah p67,93,94, Nikhil Advani p74, NTR National Award p76, New York Times p80, Nawazuddin Siddiqui p84, Namesake p87, Nargis Dutt Award p88, New York City p89, Nagesh Kukunoor p89, Nasir Abdullah p89, Naushad p99,

O - Oriya p4,8,48,49,50,51,58,59,98,135, Oscars p7,8,49,55,61,78,79,80,81,82,83,84,85,137, Oonche Log p20, O'Henry p23,30, One Night with the King p26, Onir p31, Om p55, Orissa p58, Odisha Living Legend p58, Oxford University p65, Ooty p76, Octopussy p87, Om Puri p94,94, Orissa State Film Award p98,

P - Punjab Mail p11, Paul Muni p11, Prithviraj Kapoor p13, Pukar p13,14, Prem Nagar p13, Poonam Dhillon p15, Prahaar p17, Peter D'Souza p17, Papa Kehte Hain p19, Padma Shri p14,20,26,41,139, Phani Majumdar p20, Presidency College, Kolkata p22,37,39,95,134, Pooja p24, Page3 p25, Paan Singh Tomar p26, Parineeta p27,28,139, Phool Aur Kante p29, Pinjar p30, Paa p31, Pramathesh Barua p34, Prisoner of Zenda p35, Pritish Sarkar p36,46, Paromita p39, Paromitar Ek Din p39, Podokkhep p39, Philips p39, Piya p40, Parambrata Chatterjee p40, Priyanshu Chatterjee p41, Parama p42, Papu Bhai p42, Prodip Dutta p43, Prashanta Nanda p50,98, Priyadarshan p5157, Padum Baruah p53, President's Gold Medal p55, Prakash Raj p57,66, Pather Panchali p61,64,134, Prize of the Public p64, Partho Sen Gupta p66, Pankaj Kapur p67,93, Premendra Mitra p67, President of India p69, Party p75, Peter 'O Toole p81, Prashanth p83, Phoolan Devi p84, Pradip Krishen p87,91, Pune p88, Prakash Belawadi p90, Pamela Rook p91, Paresh Rawal p93, Pritam Chakraborty p94, Prabhu Deva p95, Phula Chandana p98, Prodosh Sen p102, Prodosh Chandra Mitra p102,

Q - Qayamat Se Qayamat Tak p19, Quick Gun Murugan p98,

R - Raja Harishchandra p7,9,49, Rabindra Sangeet p12, Raj Kapoor p12,17,67,102, Ruby Myers p13, Rattan p14, Roti p14, Roop Tera Mastana p16, Ritwik Ghatak p8,16,37,39,40,82,135, Rakesh Bedi p17, Rang Birangi p17, Raja Jani p18, Ramanand Sagar p18, Rajinder Singh Bedi p19,82, Rehana Sultan p19, Rajendra Kumar p20, Radio Ceylon p20, Railway Platform p20, Raaj Kumar p20, Rock On p,30,32,75,97, Rituparno Ghosh p23,29,34,65,75,88,89, Rolling Stone p24, Royal Academy of Dramatic Art p24, Rediff p24, Raghu Romeo p24, Roshni Shekhawat p26, Ram Shankar Nikumbh p26, Rosy Miss p27, Rocky p28,

www.ingramcontent.com/pod-product-compliance
Lightning Source LLC
Chambersburg PA
CBHW061726020426
42331CB00006B/1119